BROWN V. BYRD

Second Edition

BROWN V. BYRD

Second Edition

Frank D. Rothschild

Attorney at Law
Kilauea, Hawaii

Deanne Siemer

Attorney at Law
Wilsie Co. LLC
Washington, D.C.

Anthony J. Bocchino

Professor of Law
Temple University
Beasley School of Law
Philadelphia, Pennsylvania

NATIONAL INSTITUTE FOR TRIAL ADVOCACY

Address inquiries to:
Reprint Permission
National Institute for Trial Advocacy
1685 38th Street, Suite 200
Boulder, CO 80301-2735
Phone: (800) 225-6482
Fax: (720) 890-7069
E-mail: permissions@nita.org

ISBN 978-1-60156-220-3
FBA 1220

14 13 12 11 10 9 8 7 6 5 4 3 2 1

Printed in the United States of America

CONTENTS

Fact Summary

Kenneth Brown brought suit against Robert Byrd for damages arising out of a collision between their cars on April 20, 2012, near the intersection of 12th Avenue and East Main Street in Nita City. Brown alleges that Byrd followed him too closely and failed to keep a proper lookout. Brown is seeking to recover damages for his neck, back, and head injuries, loss of wages, and pain and suffering, which he claims were caused by Byrd's negligence. Byrd denies liability and asserts that the impact was caused when Brown stopped short after initially starting through the intersection, that Byrd was contributory negligent, and in the alternative, even if the accident was his fault, the impact was not sufficient to cause, and did not cause, any physical injury to Brown.

The accident was investigated at the scene by Officer David Pierce of the Nita City Police Department. Officer Pierce was called to the scene by radio dispatch at 3:40 p.m. and conducted an investigation. He interviewed the two drivers involved in the accident and inspected the scene. The accident was, in his opinion, unavoidable. That, coupled with the fact that there were no injuries either visible or complained of by either party, resulted in no citations being issued.

Brown alleges that as a result of being rear-ended by Byrd's car he suffered back, neck and head injuries. He further claims that the injury prevents him from engaging in any strenuous exercise or activity, and that the muscle relaxant prescription drugs he is required to take prevent him from drinking any alcoholic beverages, even beer. Brown asserts that his injuries, his pain and suffering, and the deprivation of his activities warrant substantial compensation. Brown is also asking for lost wages.

Byrd's insurance carrier asked one of its investigators, David Randolf, to review and verify Brown's alleged injuries. After an investigation, Randolf filed a report with the insurance carrier disputing the extent of the injuries claimed by Brown. Randolf began his investigation by identifying Brown by reference to a picture provided by the insurance company and by setting up a surveillance of Brown's home on June 24, 2012. He noted no unusual activity on the first day of the surveillance. On June 25, Randolf followed Brown to the Nita Country Club. This was just over two months after Brown's alleged injury. At that time, Randolf observed Brown play two sets of tennis and then consume four or five beers, both at the tennis court and at the nearby outdoor patio bar. Randolf took photographs of Brown playing tennis and drinking beer.

IN THE DISTRICT COURT OF THE FIFTH CIRCUIT
STATE OF NITA

KENNETH BROWN,	)	
	)	
Plaintiff,	)	
	)	
v.	)	CIVIL NO. 2892
	)	
ROBERT BYRD,	)	
	)	
Defendant.	)	
	)	

COMPLAINT

COMES NOW the Plaintiff, Kenneth Brown, and for his cause of action against Defendant, Robert Byrd, alleges and avers as follows:

1. At all times material herein, Kenneth Brown was a resident of the City of Nita, State of Nita.

2. Upon information and belief, Defendant, Robert Byrd, was a citizen and resident of the State of Nita at all times material herein.

3. On or about April 20, 2012, Plaintiff was driving a 2003 Honda Civic LX sedan south bound on 12th Avenue in the vicinity where it intersects with East Main Street in Nita City, Nita.

4. As the traffic light turned yellow in Plaintiff's direction at the intersection of 12th Avenue and East Main Street, he stopped his vehicle.

5. As Plaintiff stopped a 2010 Toyota Camry sedan driven by Defendant slammed into the rear of Plaintiff's car.

6. As a direct and proximate result of the negligence of Defendant in failing to stop, following too closely, failing to keep a proper lookout, being inattentive, and otherwise driving in a negligent manner, Plaintiff has suffered multiple injuries for which he must take pain medication; mental and emotional distress; loss of enjoyment of life; and pain and suffering. Plaintiff has also become unable to engage in strenuous work or exercise.

7. As a further direct and proximate result of the negligence of Defendant, Plaintiff has suffered lost income and earning capacity, and incurred past and future medical and rehabilitative expenses, all in an amount which exceeds the tort threshold set forth in Chapter 431 of the Nita Revised Statutes.

WHEREFORE, Plaintiff prays for relief as follows:

(1) That judgment be entered against Defendant in an amount to be determined at trial.

(2) That Plaintiff be awarded his special damages in an amount to be determined at trial.

(3) That Plaintiff be awarded his general damages in an amount to be determined at trial.

(4) That Plaintiff be awarded his costs and such other relief as this Court deems just and proper.

DATED: June 1, 2012, Nita City, Nita.

Harriet Cooperman
Harriet Cooperman
Attorney for Plaintiff

Harriet Cooperman
Nita City Tower, Suite 201
5 Main Street
Nita City, NI 99992
555-726-6269
Nita Bar No. 10848

IN THE DISTRICT COURT OF THE FIFTH CIRCUIT
STATE OF NITA

KENNETH BROWN,	)	
	)	
Plaintiff,	)	
	)	
v.	)	CIVIL NO. 2892
	)	
ROBERT BYRD,	)	
	)	
Defendant.	)	
	)	

ANSWER

COMES NOW Defendant, Robert Byrd, by and through his attorney, Law Offices of Timothy Halbrock, and for an answer to the Complaint filed on June 1, 2012 alleges and avers as follows:

1. Defendant is without knowledge or information sufficient to form a belief as to the truth of the allegations contained in Paragraphs 1 and 3 of the Complaint and therefore Defendant leaves Plaintiff to his proof.

2. Defendant admits the allegations contained in Paragraph 2 of the Complaint.

3. Defendant denies the allegations contained in Paragraphs 4, 5, 6 and 7 of the Complaint.

FIRST AFFIRMATIVE DEFENSE

If Plaintiff received any of the injuries or suffered any of the damages as alleged in the Complaint, such injuries or damages were caused in whole or in part or contributed to by the negligence of Plaintiff.

SECOND AFFIRMATIVE DEFENSE

That pursuant to Section 663-31 of the Nita Revised Statutes, Defendant alleges that the negligence of Plaintiff was greater than the negligence, if any, of Defendant.

THIRD AFFIRMATIVE DEFENSE

Defendant hereby gives notice that apportionment of damages for prior and subsequent injuries may be used as affirmative defenses.

WHEREFORE, Defendant prays as follows:

(1) That the Complaint herein be dismissed against Defendant and that he be awarded his costs herein.

(2) That Defendant has such other and further relief as this Court deems just and equitable in the premises.

DATED: July 8, 2012, Nita City, Nita.

Timothy Halbrock

Timothy Halbrock
Attorney for Defendant

Timothy Halbrock
1100 Ward Avenue, Suite 212
Nita City, NI 99992
555-482-5879
Nita Bar No. 34686

DEPOSITION SUMMARY OF KENNETH BROWN

My name is Ken Brown and I am thirty-three years old. I am single. For the past ten years I have worked as an institutional stockbroker here in Nita City at Golden Investments, located at 637 12th Avenue. I live at 5 Scott Place in the southern part of town. I grew up here and graduated from South Central Nita High School. I was on the swim and tennis teams while in high school and concentrated on tennis while in college, competing on the collegiate level at UCLA where I played both singles and doubles. Even though I was not good enough to turn pro, tennis played a big part in my life after that, not only because I like the game and it helps me keep in shape, but also because it opened a lot of doors for me professionally in landing accounts and keeping customers happy. I joined the Nita Country Club soon after taking my current position with Golden Investments.

On April 20, 2012, I was driving home at the time of the accident. I had left work a little early. My normal hours are 5:30 a.m. to 3:30 p.m. I have to be at work before 6 a.m. because the stock market opens at 9:30 a.m. East Coast time, which is 6:30 a.m. out here. Walt Wilkins, who handles after-hours trading, came in about 2:30 p.m. to cover for me and I briefed him about where the market stood when it closed at 4 p.m. East Coast time and what we traded up to that point. I have known Walt since college. He was my doubles partner on the tennis team. At any rate, I left shortly after 3:00 p.m. or so. My office is just six blocks up 12th Avenue from Main Street, and I take the same route every day when I head home. I am always especially careful as I near Main Street because the elementary school is right on the corner and a lot of youngsters are out and about at the school using the playground all year-round. On the day of the accident the school was just letting out at around 3:15 or 3:30, and there were a lot of kids out. There were also some crossing guards, and I think there was an ice cream truck on one corner of the intersection. As I approached the intersection I was extra cautious because of the kids in the area. The light was green so I intended to go through the intersection.

I was traveling south at no more than twenty miles per hour as I approached the intersection. Just before I got to the crosswalk the light turned yellow. Because I travel this same street five days a week, I know this light has an especially quick yellow. At the same time I saw a kid running towards the intersection near the crossing guard. Because of the shortness of the yellow light and the kid, I knew I would never be able to safely make it through the intersection, so I applied my brakes and stopped almost immediately. I didn't realize the clown behind me had sped up from a safe distance to right on my tail, and the instant I stopped he smashed into my car.

1.   Q.   Where was your car, in relation to the crosswalk, when you were hit?

2.   A.   I had just come up to the crosswalk.

3.   Q.   No part of your car was in the crosswalk at all?

4.   A.   I was just into the crosswalk when I got smashed, but he pushed me through the

5.   crosswalk and into the intersection.

6.   Q.   Where was the front of your car in relation to the crosswalk when you got out of

7.   the car?

8.   A.   I was just through the crosswalk into the intersection.

9.   Q.   How far did your car move forward after you were hit from behind?

10. A.   I'm not sure, the width of the crosswalk, maybe ten feet.

I will draw on this diagram you have given me the approximate location my Honda was when it was hit from behind. I drew a rectangle and put the word Honda written beside it. I also drew in the Toyota. I have also shown where I saw the kid and the crossing guard by marking it with an X. I have marked that as Exhibit 13 as you requested.

I didn't feel hurt at all after the accident. It's funny how you hear about other people in accidents who feel fine with the rush of adrenalin right afterwards, and only later start to feel bad. That's what happened to me. It only started to hurt that night while I was in an out-of-town hotel on a business trip. The police officer was there in a matter of minutes, and I told him I felt fine and didn't need any medical assistance. It was obvious who was at fault because the other guy rear-ended me. When it came to explaining what actually happened, the officer didn't have time for us. He spent ten minutes getting down all the basic information like name, address, license numbers and so on, but then he got called to another accident and left. We never got to tell him what happened. I was shocked that he didn't give Byrd a ticket. He just rushed off without fully investigating our accident. He seemed like a real rookie, too. Nice enough guy, but still wet behind the ears, if you know what I mean. He couldn't have been older than twenty or twenty-one.

The next day my neck and back got worse and worse. I was in so much pain I went to see my doctor, Dr. Gomez. It hurt so much that I had to have Walt Wilkins drive me to the appointment. Dr. Gomez sent me to the hospital to get an X-ray and an MRI. I was told that they didn't show anything other than some degenerated disc problems at L4-5. The doctor told me that this was probably from years of playing tennis and probably not from the accident. He said that there was little he could do for me and recommended that I rest and take ibuprofen for the pain. I decided I'd see a chiropractor, Dr. McCullough, who has an office in his house near my home. Dr. McCullough recommended we treat the condition conservatively, meaning with regular adjustments, hot baths, ibuprofen, and massage for the first week. When this didn't do much to relieve the pain that first week, he then prescribed the muscle relaxants that I've been taking ever since just to marginally function. I also got a prescription for pain medication for when it just got too much to handle, but I use them sparingly. I also had some really bad headaches for a few weeks and got dizzy spells for a short time. The headaches came on about every afternoon. I only get a headache now about once a week.

It was very difficult for me mentally as well, trying to handle the loss of my physical life, and wondering if my back problem would ever go away so I could feel normal again. The nights were the worst time because I found it hard to find a comfortable position and I didn't sleep nearly as soundly as I used to. And I would wake up stiff as a board, and have to take pills all day to make it through.

<u>Page 22</u>

8.   Q.   How have you been feeling lately, Mr. Brown?

9.   A: In the past two months I have had some improvement and although I still can't

10.   play tennis, I can do the stretching I used to do religiously every morning, and

11.   I'm getting better.

My back gave me problems at work as well. I often had to work standing up. Since I've been stretching regularly in the past several months, I've been okay at work. I do get tired a lot faster than I used to. By the end of work, it's all I can do to get home and put my feet up to rest. I am hopeful that I'll be able to start playing tennis again in the future. Dr. McCullough says I've made progress, and if I continue my treatments tennis is not out of the question, although I'll probably never get back to the level I was at before the accident. Overall, I'd say my back is about 80 percent of what it was before the accident. The real problems lasted for about six months, and since then I've been making pretty steady progress.

1.   Q.   Do you drink alcohol?

2.   A.   Not now I don't.

3.   Q.   What about before the accident, did you drink then?

4.   A.   Well, I never have been a big drinker. I would have an occasional beer or two

5.   after work with a client or friend, or often after playing tennis, or wine with a

6.   date. Nothing much.

7.   Q.   Would you drink three or four beers in one get-together?

8.   A.   No, just one or two at the most.

9.   Q.   After the accident, did you drink at all?

10.   A.   No, that's been cut out of my life as well because of strict orders from my doctor

11.   not to mix alcohol with my medications. I've also been told that the alcohol can

12.   affect my headaches and memory loss.

13.   Q.   Have you followed those orders exactly at all times?

14.   A.   I followed those orders to a tee. I don't drink at all anymore, not even beer.

15.   Q.   You never drink anything alcoholic now, not even a beer or two?

16.   A.   No, I don't. I can't drink so much as a single beer on this medication.

Yes, these photos marked as Exhibits 5, 6, 7, and 8 are pictures of me playing tennis. I recognize the court as one at the country club. Yes, these photos marked as Exhibits 9, 10, and 11 are pictures of me drinking a beer. Exhibit 12 looks like just outside on the courts. Also at the club. So what.

18.   Q: Showing you what have been marked as Exhibits 5, 6, 7 and 8, who took these

19.   pictures of you playing tennis?

20.   A: I have no idea when they were taken. They couldn't have been taken since the

21.   accident because, like I said, I haven't been able to play tennis or drink.

22.   Q: What about Exhibits 9, 10, 11, and 12?

23.   A: The three are pictures of me drinking beer and Exhibit 12 looks just like outside

24.   our tennis courts.

No, you're right, there was that one time just a couple months after the accident when I foolishly tried to see if I could handle a game of tennis. I was so frustrated that I just had to try and play. I missed it so much. I played with my doubles partner, Walter Wilkins, who I also work with. I took a bunch of muscle relaxants and I felt okay during the couple of sets we played. I was so excited I probably had a few beers just to celebrate being back out on the courts and feeling so alive. Walt had driven, so I wasn't worried about driving home. But I paid for it later that day and for a couple of weeks after. My chiropractor, Dr. McCullough, was really upset with me and said I probably set my treatment back a month. But that was the one and only time I tested myself that way. I learned my lesson the hard way. Yes, Exhibit 21 is my final bill from Dr. McCullough.

This accident has also hurt me financially. I was not as good at my job during 2012 because I was distracted by pain. I was the top earner in my group in 2011 and I made a little over $450,000. In 2012, I was eighteenth out of twenty people in the group and made over $125,000 less than in 2011. My income for 2012 was approximately $325,000, as compared to $450,000 in 2011. Fortunately I have been feeling better this year and my earnings are back up, so I'm currently second in the group for 2013.

I took my car into the shop a few weeks after the accident to have the bumper repaired. I thought they could fix it, but instead they wound up putting on a whole new bumper. It was expensive. Exhibit 19 is a copy of the bill, which I paid.

You have shown me a set of notes marked as Exhibit 3 and I recognize it as notes I kept of times when I felt pain after the accident. I made these using the notes app on my smart phone. They aren't complete because I didn't start doing it until I was advised to do so two weeks after the accident by my lawyer. I wasn't always diligent in making notes. You have also shown me a document marked as Exhibit 4. I recognize Exhibit 4 as the first quarter 2012 work evaluation I received at my job at Golden Investments. I don't agree with the evaluation, but it is what I received from my supervisor, Alyssa Hoffman.

I have read this deposition, and it is complete and accurate.

Kenneth Brown

Kenneth Brown
January 4, 2013

DEPOSITION SUMMARY OF ROBERT BYRD

My name is Bob Byrd. I am thirty-five years old and I live at 104 East Main Street in Nita City. I am married and have two children, Mike, age eight, and David, age six. I work as a salesperson for an auto parts supply company, Nita Automart. I have been sued by Kenneth Brown for a car accident I had with him.

<u>Page 18</u>

1.   Q: Where were you going at the time of the accident?

2.   A: I had an appointment at Ferguson Auto Body.

3.   Q: Where is that located?

4.   A: In South Nita City.

5.   Q: What time was the appointment?

6.   A: Four.

7.   Q: Why were you going there?

8.   A: They're a client of mine. I had an appointment to meet with the Parts Manager,

9.   Bill Cheswick. He's hard to get an appointment with.

10.   Q: How long does it take to get to Ferguson's from where the accident happened?

11.   A: I know I was cutting it close, but if it wouldn't have been for this accident,

12.   I would have gotten there in time.

As I said, the accident involved a man, who I now know as Ken Brown, at the intersection of 12th and East Main in Nita City on April 20, 2012. The accident occurred at 3:30 in the afternoon. The weather was clear and dry.

As I approached the intersection of 12th and Main, I was traveling south on 12th Avenue at about 25 miles per hour, which is the speed limit on that part of 12th. Mr. Brown's Honda sedan was about two car lengths ahead of me.

The light was green but Brown slowed a bit as he came to the intersection. On the northwest corner of that intersection is the Nita Elementary School. Because school was letting out at that time, I was being especially careful watching the school children near the intersection on the northwest corner. I saw a crossing guard bending over and talking to a little boy, who looked like my David, on the northeast corner of the intersection. There were also some children, I'd estimate about eight or ten of them, crowded around an ice cream truck parked just east of the intersection, facing west on East Main Street.

<u>Page 35</u>

1.   Q: Tell me how the accident happened.

2.   A: I was driving behind Mr. Brown's car, maybe fifteen feet behind him, going no

3.   more than twenty. When I got about twenty feet from the crosswalk on 12th, the

4.   light turned yellow. By then I was ten feet behind him because he had slowed

5.   some. I looked and his brake lights were off and he seemed to be speeding up,

6.   so I assumed Mr. Brown would continue through the intersection.

7.   Q: Where was Mr. Brown's car at the time the light turned yellow?

8.   A: Just into the crosswalk.

9.   Q: Not into the intersection?

10.   A: Well just about.

11.   Q: But not there yet?

12.   A: Not yet, but I assumed he would continue through.

13.   Q: Why did you make that assumption?

14.   A: It was the only intelligent thing to do.

15.   Q: Why's that?

16.   A: Well, otherwise he would have to have jammed on his brakes and stop suddenly.

17.   Q: What's wrong with that?

18.   A: Obviously, it can cause someone following behind to run into you.

19.   Q: Which is what you did?

20.   A: My point exactly.

21.   Q: Had Mr. Brown continued as you assumed, what were you going to do?

22.   A: I planned to follow him right through the intersection. In my opinion, it was safer

23.   to go through the light, even if it changed while I was in the intersection, than

24.   jamming on my brakes.

25.   Q: Even if the light turned red?

26.   A: Yes, even if it turned red.

At any rate, I glanced left and right as I got to the intersection. Instead of going through, Brown suddenly slammed on the brakes and stopped. He must have been almost through the crosswalk when he braked. That's why I thought he was going through. I hit the brakes as hard as I could, but I still ran into the rear end of Brown's car. I have marked on this diagram the location of Brown's car and the location of my car when the impact happened. I'm sure Brown was through the crosswalk and into the intersection when I hit him. I may not have these exactly to scale, though. I marked this as Exhibit 14 and I signed it as you have asked. When I hit him, I was doing no more than ten miles per hour. In fact, the damage to my car, a 2010 Toyota, was minimal. There was a hardly noticeable ding in the back of Brown's Honda. The impact was so minimal that neither of our air bags deployed.

Brown jumped out of his car and came towards me. I asked him why he stopped short, and he said he had a red light and the wreck was all my fault. I didn't want to get into an argument with him, so I didn't respond, but to my way of thinking, this accident was his fault. It is unsafe to stop so quickly. The yellow light is a caution light, not a stop light, and he should have driven appropriately and gone through the intersection with caution especially when he didn't brake until the last possible second after he was in the crosswalk. I did ask him if he was hurt and he said that he wasn't.

A cop came and investigated the accident. I told him I couldn't avoid hitting Brown. He obviously agreed with me because I didn't get a ticket.

About a week later I took my car into the repair shop to get an estimate for fixing my front bumper. Because the damage was so slight, and the repair cost so high, I decided to leave the car as it was. The estimate from Nita City Collision Center for $581.66 is Exhibit 20.

I have read this deposition, and it is complete and accurate.

Robert Byrd

Robert Byrd
January 7, 2013

DEPOSITION SUMMARY OF OFFICER DAVID PIERCE

I am David Pierce, patrol officer for the Nita City Police Department. I am twenty-five years old and have been on the force two years. On April 20, 2012, I received a dispatch at approximately 3:40 p.m. to proceed to the intersection of 12th Avenue and East Main for a reported accident. I arrived within five minutes and noted a two-car accident involving a rear-end collision in the southbound lane of 12th Avenue at around the north crosswalk. The drivers of the two cars, whom I later identified to be Kenneth Brown and Robert Byrd, were standing on the sidewalk by the elementary school. I first spoke with the drivers to determine the extent of any injuries in order to decide whether an ambulance would be necessary. Neither appeared injured nor did either complain of injuries. Both were cooperative and reasonably calm. No ambulance was called.

I then surveyed the accident itself, noting that a Toyota sedan driven by Mr. Byrd had struck the rear bumper of a Honda sedan driven by Mr. Brown. Both vehicles were drivable. It was a clear, sunny day. I made notes of the standard information such as license plate and vehicle registration, date and time, insurance coverage, home addresses.

Then, as I was about to interview each driver separately, I received a message from dispatch that a twenty-car pileup had just occurred on the nearby interstate. There were several serious injuries reported, and I was directed to proceed to that location ASAP. As a result, I left the scene without fully investigating the accident and only took brief statements from each driver. I did not actually prepare my official accident report until the following day since most of my time that day was taken up with the accident on the interstate.

What I recall of the driver statements is consistent with what I noted in my report. Exhibit 1 is that report. As Mr. Brown approached the intersection on a green light, it reportedly changed to yellow. I know from my own experience that the light at that intersection has a quick yellow, but there's no way to know that unless you've been there numerous times. I am not sure exactly where he said he was located when that happened. What I do remember is Mr. Brown conveying was that he decided to stop rather than proceed through the intersection on a yellow light. No, he did not say anything about a child running towards the crosswalk. If he had, I'm sure I would recall that. Mr. Byrd was reportedly driving at or below the speed limit of twenty-five miles per hour when, in his view, Mr. Brown suddenly and without warning came to a rapid stop. Mr. Byrd had assumed that Brown would be going through the intersection because his brake lights were not on as he was going into the crosswalk area. Byrd couldn't stop fast enough, and his front bumper struck the rear bumper of Brown's car. Damage was minimal, which further corroborated the slow speed of the Byrd vehicle. Brown's car ended up in the intersection.

Yes, I realize that the driver behind in such situations is usually considered at fault. I did not issue any citations in part because the damage was slight, neither party seemed injured, and while Mr. Byrd may have been following closer than is prudent, Mr. Brown made the accident unavoidable by stopping when it appeared, from what I heard, that he should have continued through the intersection. Also, after hearing about the accident on the interstate, I simply needed to finish up with my investigation and proceed as rapidly as possible to what was obviously a more urgent situation. Perhaps if I would have had more time to talk with the parties and weigh the situation I might have issued a citation to Mr. Byrd, but I doubt it.

Neither party showed any signs of intoxication and thus that was categorically ruled out as a possible cause of the accident. I don't recall what Mr. Byrd looked like, but I do remember Mr. Brown somewhat because he was tall, lanky, and looked like a real jock. What I mean is he had the body of an athlete.

Yes, this diagram that has been marked as Exhibit 15 looks like the intersection back when this accident took place and accurately shows where the crosswalks are. Since you've asked me to draw in where the two cars ended up as I saw them when I arrived, I have drawn a box and put the letter "H" for the Honda driven by Mr. Brown, and another box behind it with the letter "T" for the Toyota driven by Mr. Byrd. I believe this drawing accurately shows where the cars were relative to the crosswalk on 12th Avenue when I arrived. Of course, I am only going from memory because I didn't make a drawing or sketch at the scene so I may be a little off.

I have read this deposition, and it is complete and accurate.

David Pierce
____

David Pierce
January 8, 2013

DEPOSITION SUMMARY OF DAVID RANDOLF

My name is David Randolf. I am forty-three years old and work as an investigator for Nita Insurance Company. The biggest lines of insurance our company writes are auto, fire, and casualty. My job for the past six years has been to investigate claims made under such policies by and against our insureds. In this capacity I was asked to conduct a surveillance of Kenneth Brown who was involved in an automobile collision with Robert Byrd and to review and verify the alleged injuries. I was told Mr. Brown was claiming to have a serious back injury as a result of a rear-end collision in downtown Nita on April 20, 2012. Apparently he claimed to be an avid tennis player and that the accident had caused such back pain that he was unable to play tennis. To assist in this investigation I was provided with a photograph of a man I was told was Mr. Brown.

I set up surveillance at Mr. Brown's home address, 5 Scott Place, on June 24, 2012. No unusual activity was noted that day. On June 25, Mr. Brown left his house carrying what appeared to be a covered tennis racket and got into a car I now know belongs to a Walter Wilkins. I followed him to the Nita Country Club out in Nita Heights. After a time in the locker room, Mr. Brown reappeared in tennis clothing and, carrying that same racket, headed out to the tennis courts adjacent to the clubhouse. I took up position in the bushes next to the court on which he was playing, as shown in the photograph you have just shown me, which is marked as Exhibit 11. My intent was to see without being seen. I had my small but powerful digital zoom camera with me to take pictures of any significant activity. The camera is capable of taking digital video as well, but I did not use that function in this surveillance.

I watched Mr. Brown play two vigorous sets of tennis and managed to take a few pictures of him in action at various stages of the game. He seemed to move effortlessly about the court, never showing any signs of stiffness or pain. I could overhear the conversations between Mr. Brown and his opponent and, while he complained of being rusty, Mr. Brown never complained of pain or impairment at all. He looked very athletic as he glided about the court, firing serves, bending for volleys, and stretching for overhead smashes. I myself have played recreational tennis for several years and am very familiar with the sport. Mr. Brown is obviously a very accomplished tennis player. If he had any back problems as of that date, it sure didn't show during the forty or so minutes I watched him play.

When I realized the second set was near to being done, I moved to another location to avoid being spotted by Mr. Brown. After the match Mr. Brown drank one or two beers at courtside, which I documented with a photograph, and then he and his playing partner went to the club's outdoor patio bar, where I saw him drink another three or four beers. I also took a photograph of him drinking at the bar. I took these photos because in my experience people with the back pain that Mr. Brown claimed to have are required to take medications that don't mix with alcohol. I again observed no signs of pain, stress, discomfort, or the like.

The eight photographs you have shown me, marked as Exhibits 5, 6, 7, 8, 9, 10, 11, and 12, are all ones I took that day. I kept the diskette used to save the photos and delivered a hard copy of the photos to the lawyer for Mr. Byrd. I did enhance the contrast of the photos before printing them, but nonetheless each photo is a true and accurate representation of what I saw that day.

I have read this deposition, and it is complete and accurate.

David Randolf

David Randolf
January 25, 2013

DEPOSITION SUMMARY OF WALTER WILKINS

My name is Walt Wilkins. I am thirty-one years old and live at 1406 Logan Court in Nita City, Nita. I work as an after-hours trader in the Institutional Stock Market for Golden Investments, also in Nita City. As such my work day normally begins at 3:00 p.m. and goes until midnight. I am single. One of my co-workers is Ken Brown. Ken and I have known each other since our college days at UCLA, where we both played on the tennis team. We both played singles, but we were best when playing together as doubles partners. We were good college players, but not good enough to turn professional. When we graduated from UCLA, we both went to work for Golden Investments and have been employed there ever since.

I know about Ken's car accident through him, and I have seen the effect it had on him. I went into work early on April 20, 2012, as a favor to Ken to cover his clients so he could catch a flight out of town that afternoon. I got in at about 2:30 p.m. Ken told me what I needed to know to cover him. He had plenty of time to get to the airport. His flight wasn't until five o'clock that night, but he had some errands to do before heading out to the airport. Ken likes to be early for flights. He likes to avoid the rush-hour traffic.

I first heard about the accident the next day. Ken emailed me at home that morning and asked if I could pick him up and take him to his doctor's office. I was pleased to help him out. Exhibit 2 is the email he sent me. When I picked him up, he looked terrible. He told me he had been rear-ended by a guy at a stoplight who obviously wasn't watching where he was going. He said he had been up most of the night at his hotel because his back and head were bothering him. He was walking all stooped over and it was obvious he was in a lot of pain. I asked him why he had gone on his trip, and he told me that he really didn't start to hurt until 2:00 a.m. when he woke up with a headache and his back in spasm.

Ken's life was much different for the rest of 2012. With one exception, he and I did not play any tennis after the accident in 2012. According to Ken, he may be allowed to play tennis in the near future. For most of 2012, Ken was pretty depressed. His back really bothered him. He hardly ever went out socially, which we used to do regularly, and I know it affected his work performance. He was the number-one broker in our group at Golden in 2011 and 2010, and he slipped to next to last in 2012. I know for a fact that his draw for 2012 alone was $60,000 less than the year before. He has been making a comeback this year and is back near the top of the group.

Yes, there was a time after the accident that Ken tried to play tennis. One Saturday, I think it was in late June, Ken called me and said he was feeling a little better and he wanted to play some tennis. I picked Ken up at his house, and he seemed to be in good spirits. He said he had taken some muscle relaxants and felt pretty good. We went to the Nita Country Club, where we both belong. We ended up playing a couple sets of tennis. Ken has always been a better player than me, relying on a big serve and great volley game. When we played that one time, he was about three-quarters speed. I toned my game down to meet his, but if I had wanted to I could have beaten him every game. His serve was nothing, and his mobility was not great, at least for him. I would be surprised if someone else described his play as anything else but mediocre, but I guess it's all about frame of reference. The way Ken was playing wasn't in the same league as his norm. After the game, we did drink a few beers, which wasn't unusual. Ken said the beer tasted particularly good, as he hadn't been able to drink since the accident. I asked him if he should slow down on the beer (I think he had maybe four or five), but he said he wasn't worried because I was the designated driver.

We made plans to go out later that evening to get something to eat, but Ken called at the last minute and cancelled. Said he had a headache. I know that he was out of work part of the next week because of his back. At any rate, that was the last time I know of that Ken tried to play tennis. He is hoping to play again, I know, and he has seemed better physically around the office. I guess he's improving.

I have read this deposition, and it is complete and accurate.

Walter Wilkins

Walter Wilkins
January 28, 2013

Jury Instructions

1. The Court will now instruct you about the law that governs this case. By your oath, you agree to accept and follow these instructions and to apply them to the facts you find from the evidence. Any verdict in this case must be the unanimous decision of all jurors.

2. The plaintiff, Kenneth Brown, claims that the defendant, Robert Byrd, negligently injured him in a motor vehicle collision in Nita City on April 20, 2012. The defendant denies that the collision caused the plaintiff any injury, and he also claims that the plaintiff negligently contributed to the cause of the collision and any injury the plaintiff sustained then.

3. Each party has the burden of proving his claim by a preponderance of the evidence, which is the greater weight of the evidence or the evidence that you find is more believable.

4. Negligence is the failure to exercise reasonable care or the care that a reasonable person would exercise under the same or similar circumstances.

5. You are the sole judges of the credibility of the witnesses and of the weight to be given to the testimony of each witness. In determining what credit is to be given any witness, you may take into account his or her ability and opportunity to observe; his or her manner and appearance while testifying; any interest, bias, or prejudice he or she may have; the reasonableness of the testimony considered in the light of all the evidence; and any other factors that bear on the believability and weight of the witness's testimony.

6. A driver must operate his vehicle in a manner that will permit him to stop without colliding with a vehicle ahead in his line of travel. A driver may enter an intersection when he faces a yellow or "caution" traffic control signal, but he has no duty to enter the intersection then if he reasonably believes that he will thereby endanger himself or others.

7. To reduce or eliminate the plaintiff's recovery for any injury, the defendant has the burden of proving that the plaintiff negligently contributed to cause that collision. In your interrogatory answers and verdict, you will determine whether the plaintiff negligently contributed to cause the collision and any injury he sustained then. If the plaintiff was more at fault than the defendant in causing the collision, your verdict should be for the defendant. If the defendant was as much or more at fault than the plaintiff in causing the collision, then the percent of fault for which the plaintiff was responsible shall reduce the plaintiff's recovery proportionately.

8. If your verdict is for the plaintiff, you should determine an amount that will fully and fairly compensate him for any injury or damage he proximately sustained in that collision, including compensation for any physical pain, emotional distress, or disability; the reasonable value of any medical care; and any loss of income he reasonably sustained. If you find with reasonable certainty that any injury he proximately sustained in that collision is permanent or will cause him future harm, you should also include an amount to compensate for that future pain, disability, or emotional distress.

IN THE DISTRICT COURT OF THE FIFTH CIRCUIT
STATE OF NITA

KENNETH BROWN,	)	
	)	
Plaintiff,	)	CIVIL NO. 2892
	)	
vs.	)	
	)	SPECIAL VERDICT FORM
ROBERT BYRD,	)	
	)	
Defendant.	)	
_______	)	

SPECIAL VERDICT FORM

The jury must answer all of the questions, unless otherwise indicated. To understand what issues are being submitted to you, you may wish to read over the entire special verdict form before proceeding to answer the questions. Answer the questions in numerical order. Follow all directions carefully. <u>Each</u> answer requires the agreement of at least ______ jurors; however, the same ______ jurors need <u>not</u> agree on each answer.

QUESTION #1: Was the Defendant negligent?

YES ______   NO ______

If your answer to Question #1 was "YES," then please go on to answer Question #2. If your answer to Question #1 was "NO," then the foreperson shall sign this document and summon the bailiff.

QUESTION #2: Was the negligence of Defendant a legal cause of Plaintiff's damages?

YES ______   NO ______

If your answer to Question #2 was "YES," then please go on to answer Question #3. If your answer to Question #2 was "NO," then the foreperson shall sign this document and summon the bailiff.

QUESTION #3: Was Plaintiff contributorily negligent?

YES ______   NO ______

If your answer to Question #3 was "YES," then please go on to answer Question #4. If your answer to Question #3 was "NO," then please skip Question #4 and Question #5 and go on to answer Question #6.

QUESTION #4: Was the contributory negligence of Plaintiff a legal cause of his damages?

YES ______   NO ______

If your answer to Question #4 was "YES," then please go on to answer Question #5. If your answer to Question #4 was "NO," then please skip Question #5 and go on to answer Question #6.

QUESTION #5: Please determine the respective negligence of Defendant and Plaintiff.

DEFENDANT   _____%

PLAINTIFF   _____%

TOTAL   _100_ %

If you answered Question #5 by assigning 50 percent or less negligence to Plaintiff, then please go on to answer Question #6. If you answered Question #5 by assigning more than 50 percent negligence to Plaintiff, then the foreperson shall sign this document and summon the bailiff.

QUESTION #6: Without reduction for Plaintiff's contributory negligence, if any, what are his total damages:

SPECIAL DAMAGES $_____

GENERAL DAMAGES $_____

TOTAL $_____

____

Foreperson

Exhibit 1

Nita City Police Department
Accident Report

1. **Investigating Officer:** D. Pierce		2. **Badge No:** 2157
3. **Date:** April 20, 2012	4. **Time:** 3:40 p.m.	5. **Place:** Nita City
VEHICLE # 1		
6. **Operator:** Kenneth Brown	7. **Address:** 5 Scott Pl. N. C.	8. **Vehicle Title #:** G18M4443798
9. **Year:** 2003	10. **Make:** Honda	11. **Model:** Civic LX Sedan
12. **Lic. Plate:** GSB 356	13. **State:** Nita	14. **Insurance:** State Farm
15. **Pol. #:** 00528-24-2234	16. **Towed:** Drivable	17. **Damage:** Rear bumper and trunk
VEHICLE # 2		
6. **Operator:** Robert Byrd	7. **Address:** 104 E. Main, N. C.	8. **Vehicle Title #:** IP644W5772
9. **Year:** 2010	10. **Make:** Toyota	11. **Model:** Camry Sedan
12. **Lic. Plate:** KJM 044	13. **State:** Nita	14. **Insurance:** Nita
15. **Pol. #:** 3001-17750-1440	16. **Towed:** Drivable	17. **Damage:** Front fender
18. **Principal Road:** 12th Avenue	19. **Speed Limit:** 25	20. **Intersecting Road:** E. Main

21. Injuries:
None - minor accident

22. Narrative:
Interviewed both drivers. Vehicle #1 was traveling south on 12th Avenue. When he neared intersection of E. Main light was green. Light changed to yellow, and #1 stopped short and was rear-ended by Vehicle #2. #2 appeared to be traveling within posted speed limit of 25 mph and to have his vehicle under control. #2 may have been following too close, but accident was made unavoidable by the sudden and unnecessary stop by #1. Note also that timing of yellow light was short as previously noted. No citations were given. Both vehicles drivable, damage minor. No injuries.

23. **Investigating Officer Signature:** David Pierce	**Date:** 4/21/2012

Exhibit 2

Ken Brown

From:	Ken Brown <Goldenboy@nitamail.nita>
Sent:	Friday, April 21, 2012 7:04 AM
To:	Walt Wilkins
Subject:	Help!

Hey Crush: can you pick me up at the airport at noon today? I need to get over to my doctor's office right away. Back and neck killing me. Had a miserable, cramped commuter flight last night to Chi-town, then got a soft, back-breaking bed at The Suites—hardly slept at all.

Reply at once. I have my Blackberry with me.

Ken

Exhibit 3

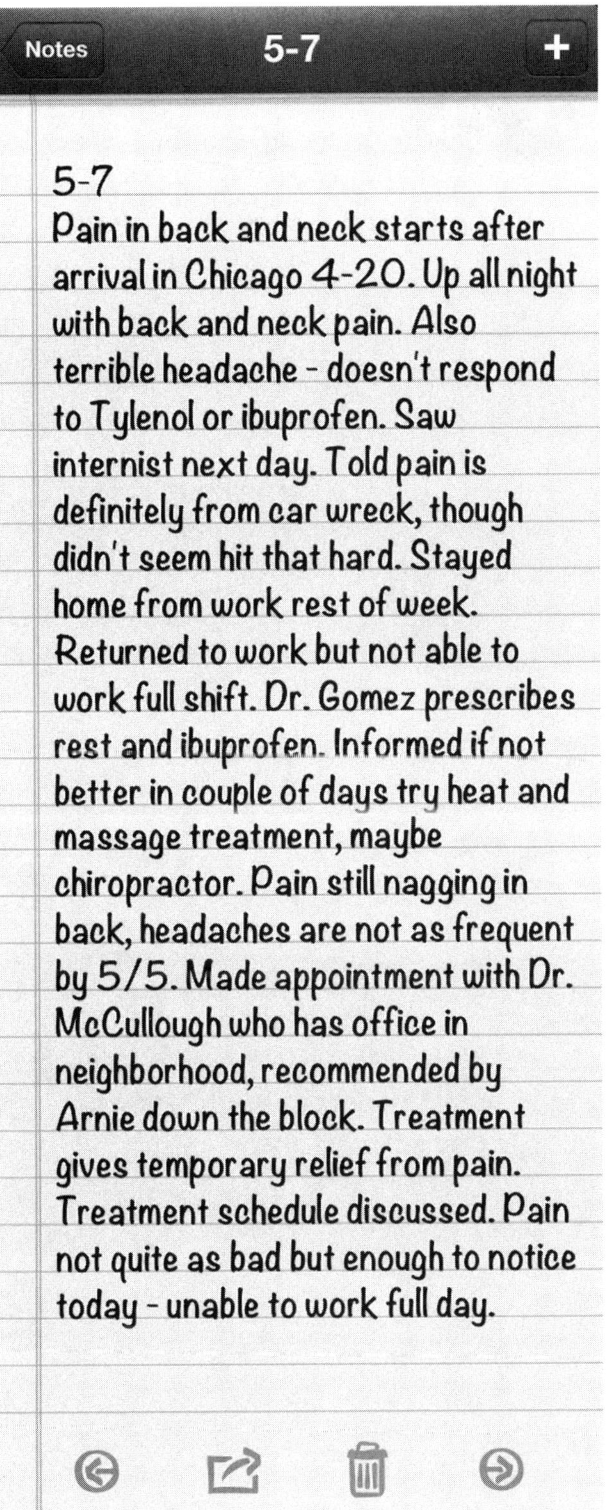
Notes
5-7
+
5-7
Pain in back and neck starts after arrival in Chicago 4-20. Up all night with back and neck pain. Also terrible headache - doesn't respond to Tylenol or ibuprofen. Saw internist next day. Told pain is definitely from car wreck, though didn't seem hit that hard. Stayed home from work rest of week. Returned to work but not able to work full shift. Dr. Gomez prescribes rest and ibuprofen. Informed if not better in couple of days try heat and massage treatment, maybe chiropractor. Pain still nagging in back, headaches are not as frequent by 5/5. Made appointment with Dr. McCullough who has office in neighborhood, recommended by Arnie down the block. Treatment gives temporary relief from pain. Treatment schedule discussed. Pain not quite as bad but enough to notice today - unable to work full day.

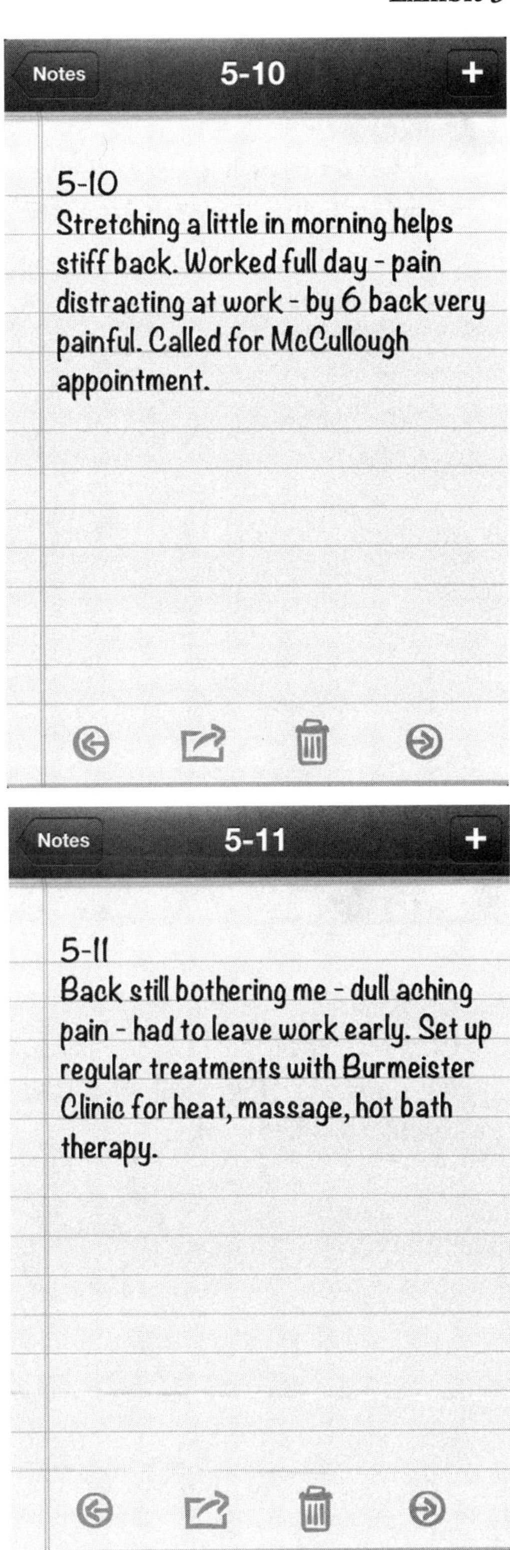
Notes
5-10
+
5-10
Stretching a little in morning helps stiff back. Worked full day - pain distracting at work - by 6 back very painful. Called for McCullough appointment.

Notes
5-11
+
5-11
Back still bothering me - dull aching pain - had to leave work early. Set up regular treatments with Burmeister Clinic for heat, massage, hot bath therapy.

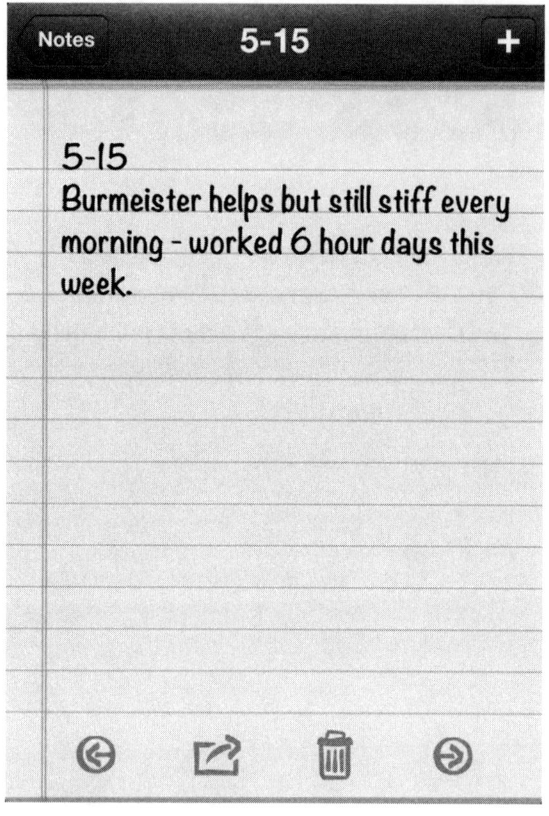

Notes   5-15   +

5-15
Burmeister helps but still stiff every
morning - worked 6 hour days this
week.

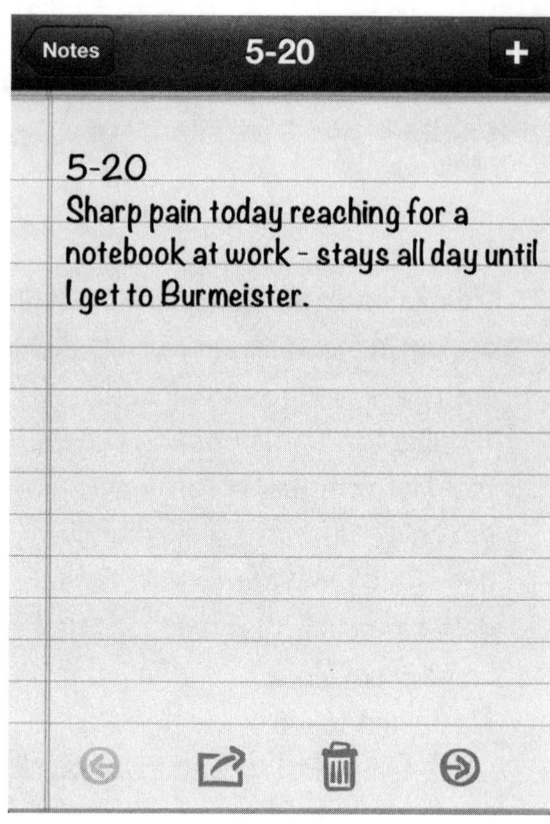

Notes   5-20   +

5-20
Sharp pain today reaching for a
notebook at work - stays all day until
I get to Burmeister.

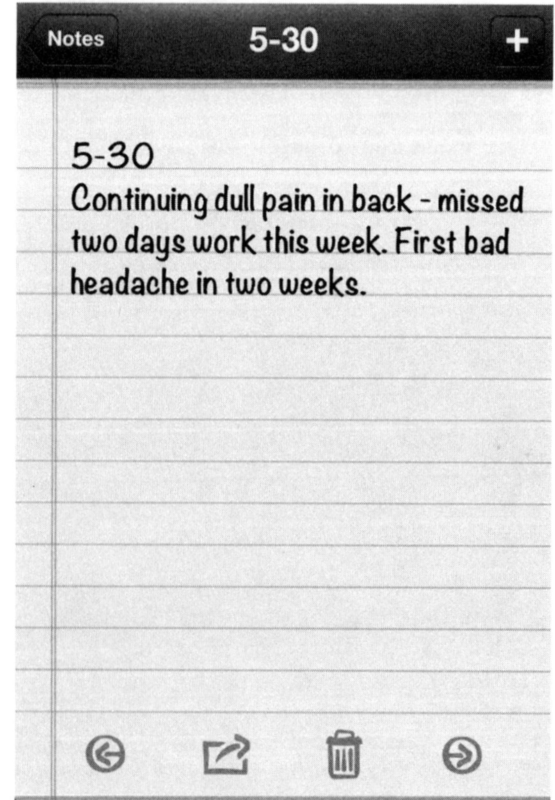

Notes   5-30   +

5-30
Continuing dull pain in back - missed
two days work this week. First bad
headache in two weeks.

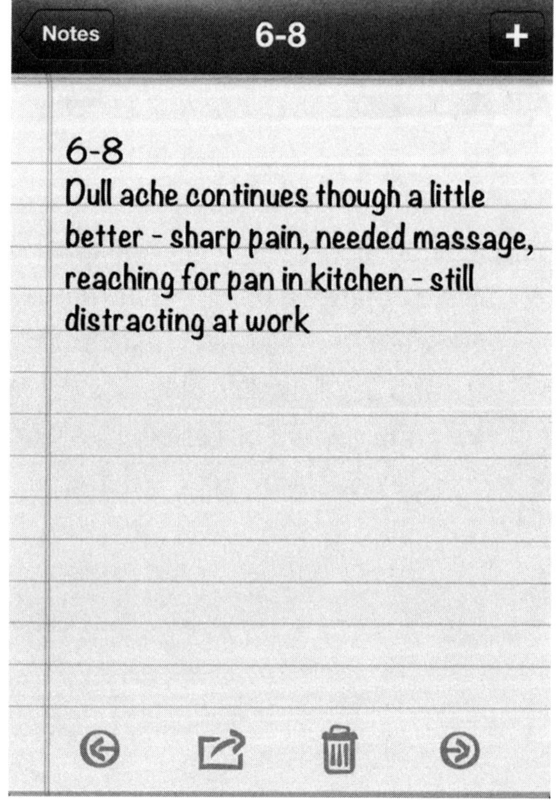

Notes   6-8   +

6-8
Dull ache continues though a little
better - sharp pain, needed massage,
reaching for pan in kitchen - still
distracting at work

Notes
6-15
+
6-15
Had a pretty good week. Back still
hurts but not as bad.

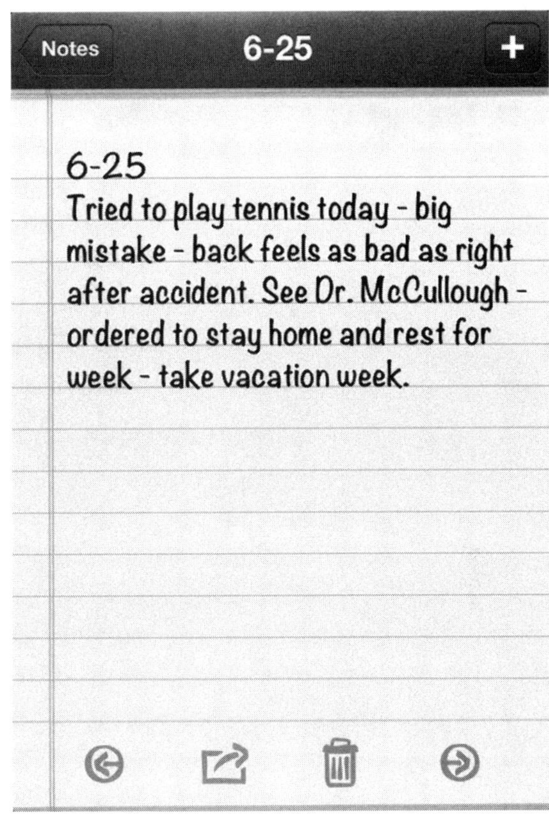
Notes
6-25
+
6-25
Tried to play tennis today - big
mistake - back feels as bad as right
after accident. See Dr. McCullough -
ordered to stay home and rest for
week - take vacation week.

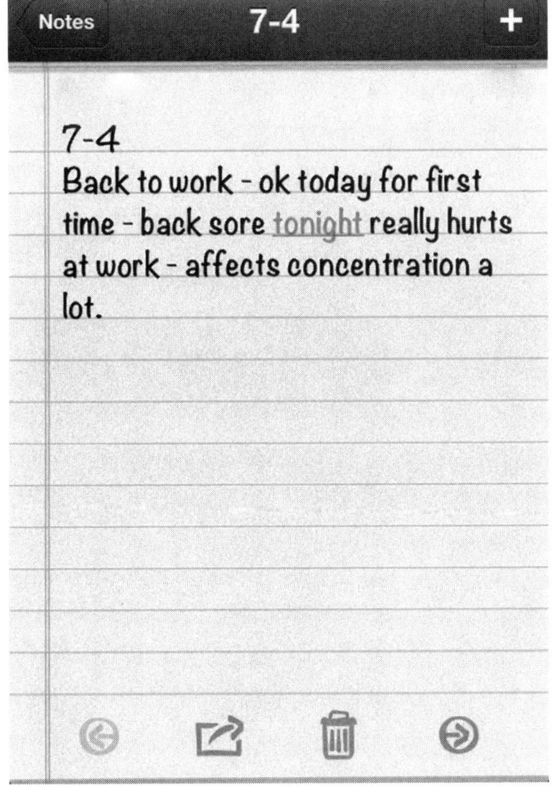
Notes
7-4
+
7-4
Back to work - ok today for first
time - back sore tonight really hurts
at work - affects concentration a
lot.

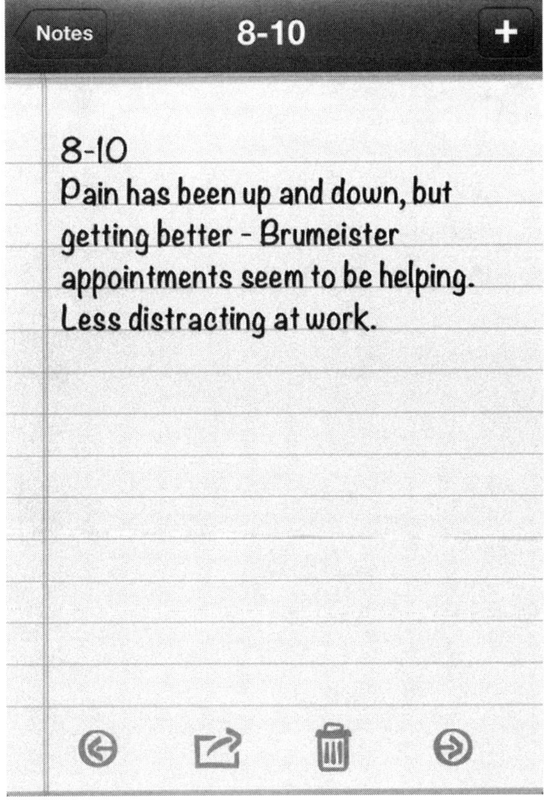
Notes
8-10
+
8-10
Pain has been up and down, but
getting better - Brumeister
appointments seem to be helping.
Less distracting at work.

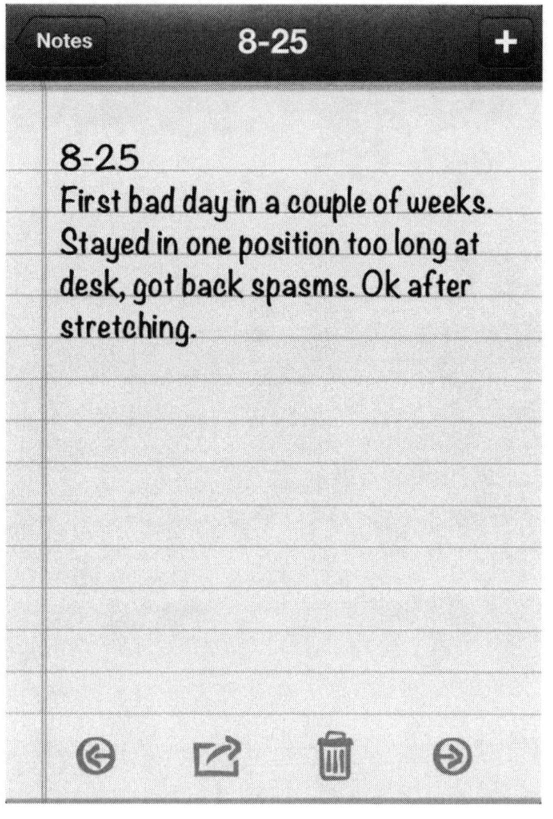

Notes
8-25
+
8-25
First bad day in a couple of weeks.
Stayed in one position too long at
desk, got back spasms. Ok after
stretching.

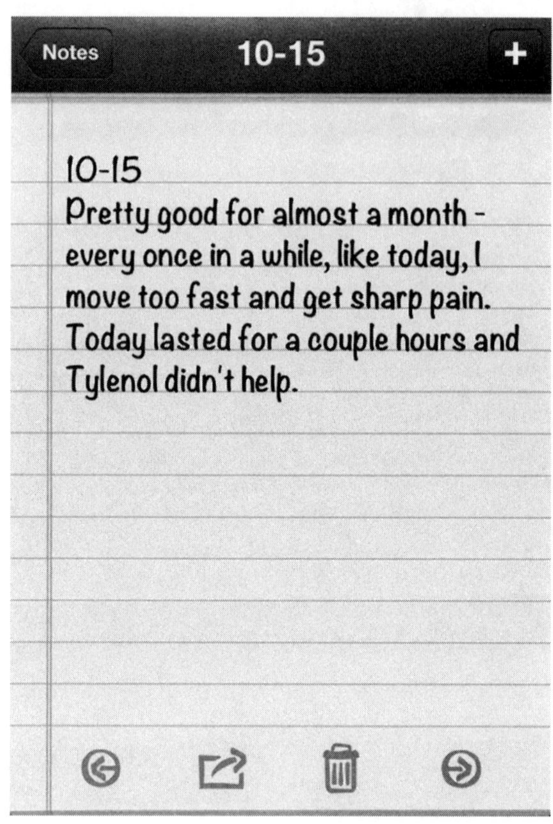

Notes
10-15
+
10-15
Pretty good for almost a month -
every once in a while, like today, I
move too fast and get sharp pain.
Today lasted for a couple hours and
Tylenol didn't help.

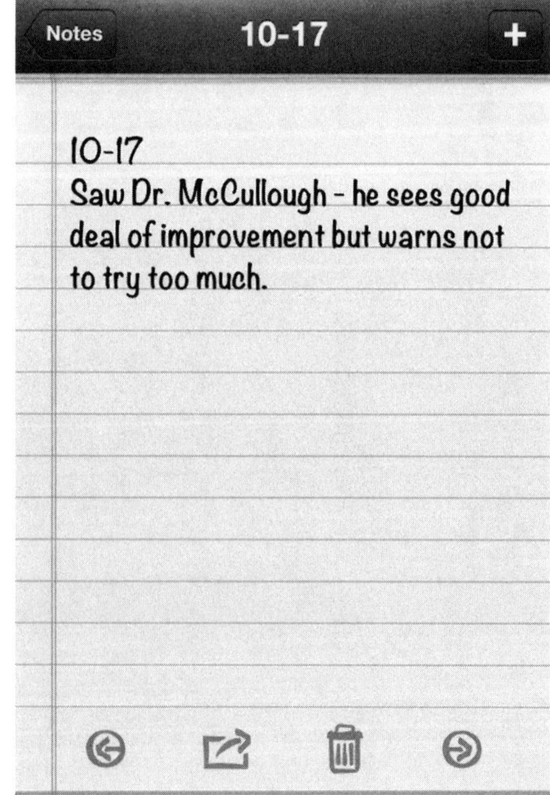

Notes
10-17
+
10-17
Saw Dr. McCullough - he sees good
deal of improvement but warns not
to try too much.

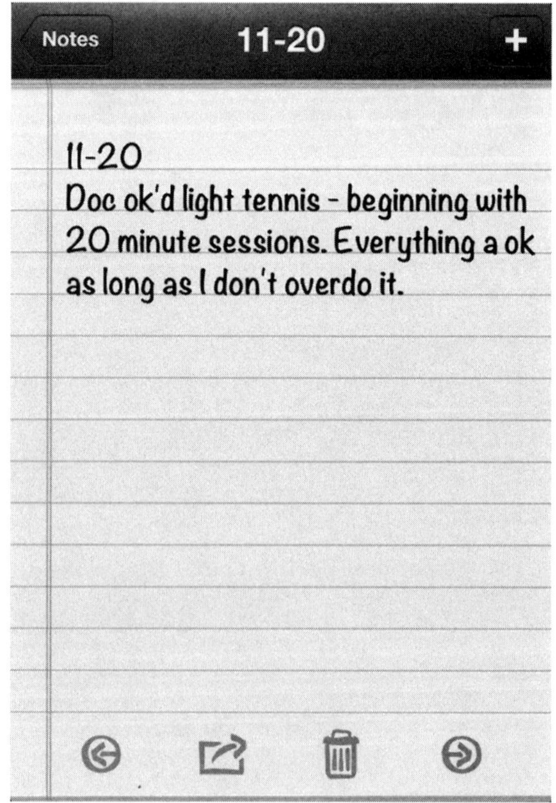

Notes
11-20
+
11-20
Doc ok'd light tennis - beginning with
20 minute sessions. Everything a ok
as long as I don't overdo it.

Exhibit 4

GOLDEN INVESTMENTS
FINANCIAL ADVISORS
MEMBER
NITA STOCK EXCHANGE
16 BULL BOULEVARD
NITA CITY, NITA

April 2, 2012

TO: Ken Brown

FROM: Alyssa Hoffman, Vice President

RE: Quarterly Review

               For the period 1/1/2012 through 3/31/2012

Salary: $20,000

Commissions: $23,256

New Clients This Quarter: 11

As the above numbers show, there is some reason for concern in your performance during the first quarter of this year. Although there has been a small slowing of the market, compared to the last quarter of 2011, your commissions for this quarter are less than half for the last quarter of 2011 when your commissions were $111,500. Similarly, while your client base was reduced by the death of your best investor, you have only 11 new customers in this quarter, when compared to the 31 new customers in the last quarter of 2011. The comparison of the first quarter of this year with the first quarter of last year is also disappointing. Your commissions for the first quarter of 2011 were $93,350 and new clients for that quarter were 23.

I am sure you share our disappointment concerning your performance, especially after your personal record year of 2012. Ken, we all go through these droughts, especially after a big year. It's time to get back to work in earnest. With your talent, I expect that you can rescue this year if you just put your mind to it. I expect that we will see significant improvements in the next quarter.

If you need any assistance, please feel free to make an appointment with my assistant.

Exhibit 5

Exhibit 6

Exhibit 7

Exhibit 8

Exhibit 10

Exhibit 11

Exhibit 12

Exhibit 13

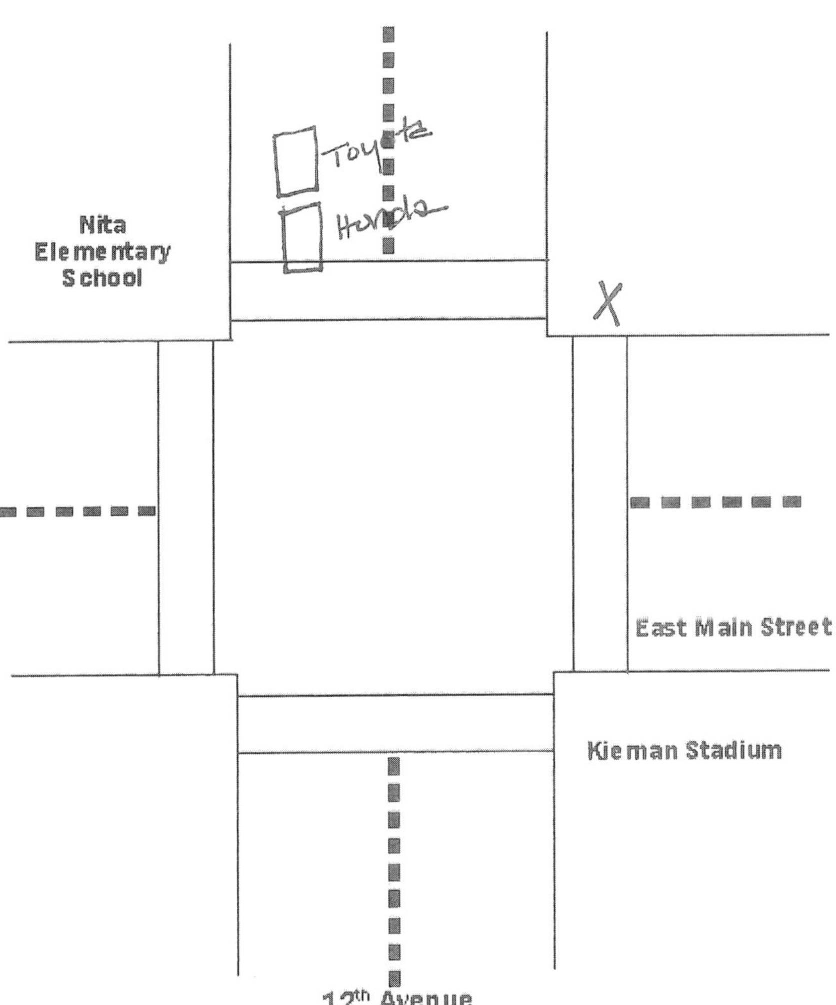

Exhibit 13

Kenneth Brown

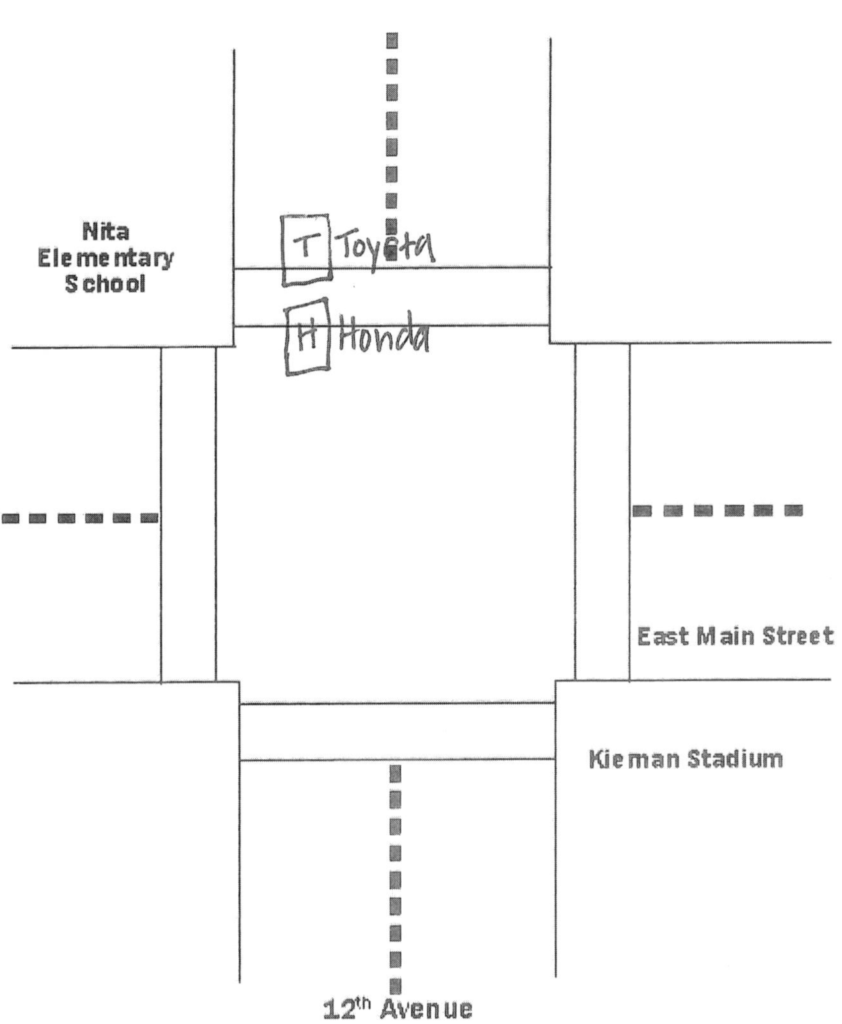

Exhibit 14
Robert Byrd

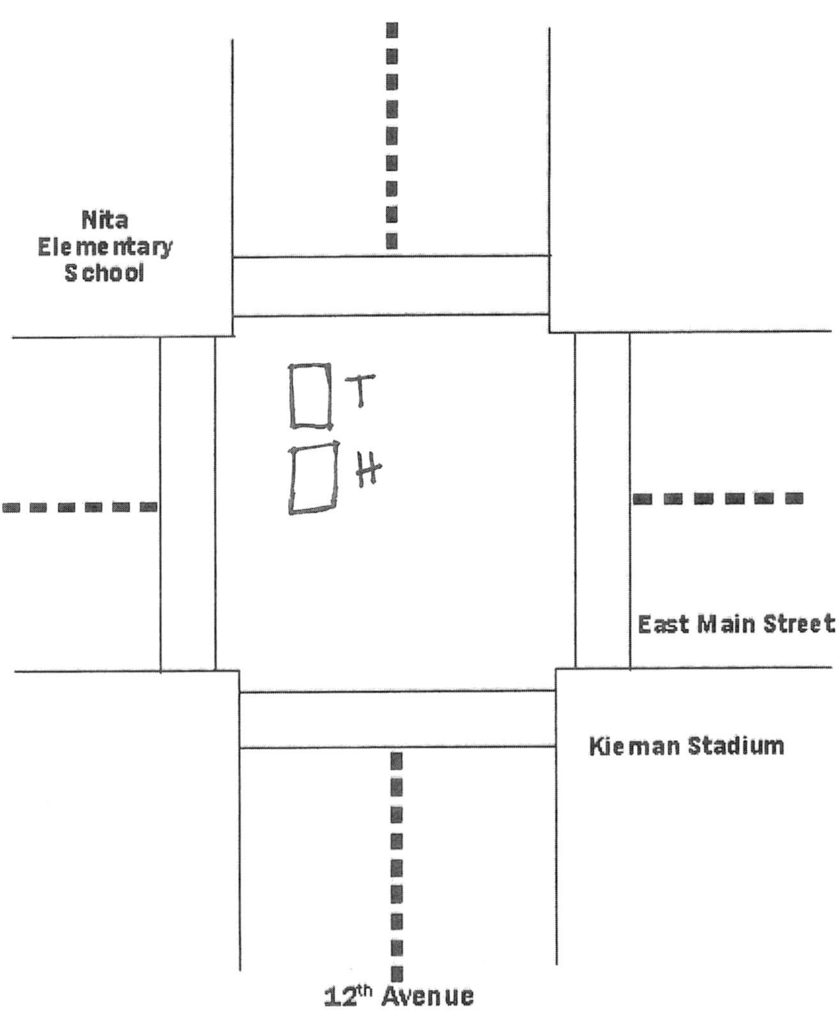

Exhibit 15
David Pierce

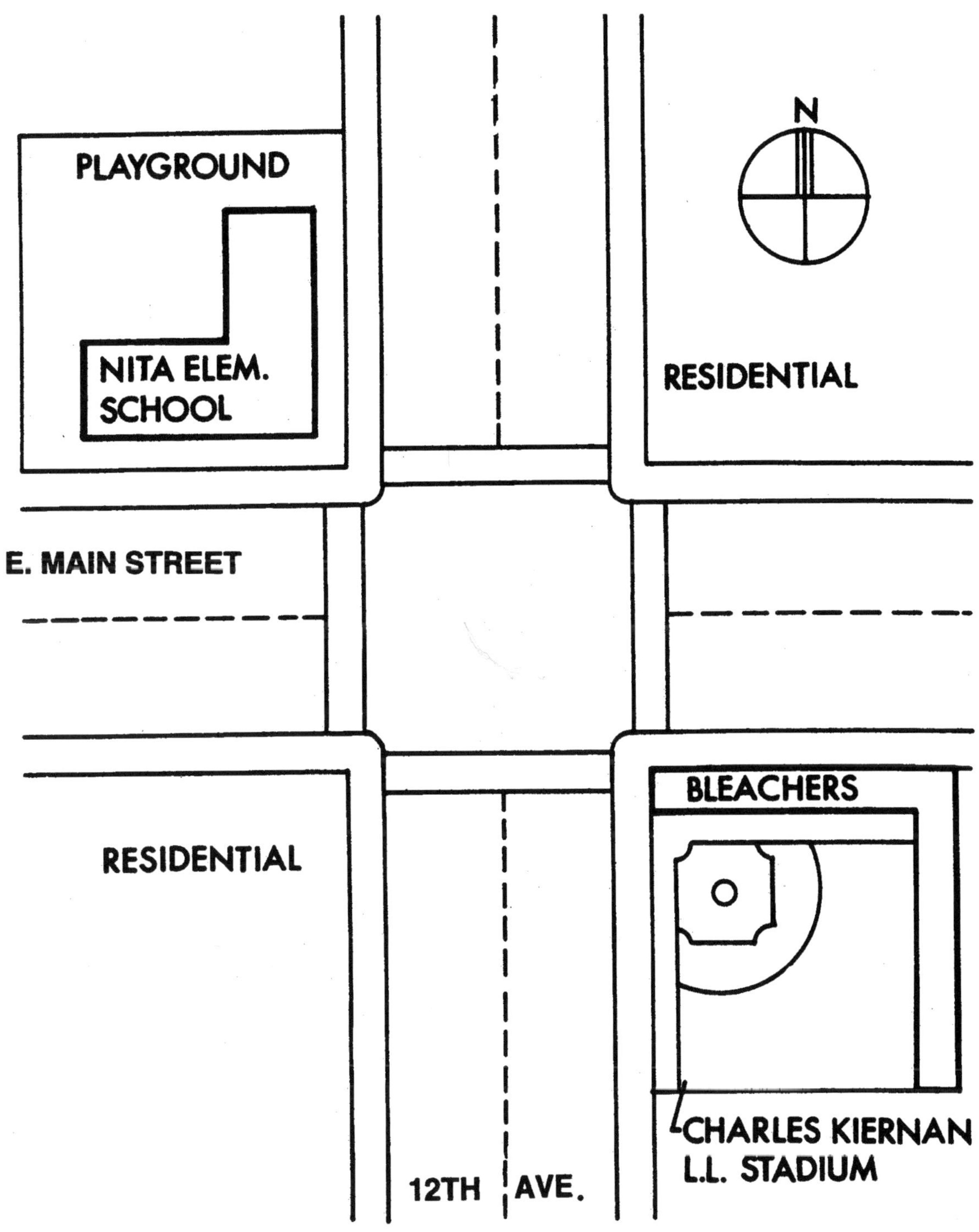

INTERSECTION — 12TH & E. MAIN

STATE OF NITA
GSB 356
CIVIC

KJM 044

Exhibit 19

NITA CITY COLLISION CENTER

3156 INDUSTRIAL WAY, NITA CITY,
NITA 99992
Phone: (808) 246-4466
FAX: (808) 246-2132

Workfile ID:	eaef9813
Federal ID:	95-4536459
License Number:	RD-3307

INVOICE [5/19/2012]

Customer: BROWN, K.

Written By: BRYAN OKINO

Insured:	Policy #:	Claim #:
Type of Loss:	Date of Loss: APRIL 20, 2012	Days to Repair: 2
Point of Impact: 06 Rear		

Owner:	Inspection Location:	Insurance Company:
BROWN, KENNETH	NITA CITY COLLISION CENTER	
5 SCOTT PLACE	3156 INDUSTRIAL WAY	
NITA CITY, NITA 99994	NITA CITY, NITA 99992	
(555) 635-6123 Cellular	Repair Facility	
	(555) 246-4466 Business	

VEHICLE

Year:	2003	Body Style:	4D SED	VIN:	2HGES16591H592621	Mileage In: 99664
Make:	HOND CIVIC LX	Engine:	4-1.7L-FI	License:	JSE-143	Mileage Out:
Model:	MAROON/RP-32P-4	Production Date:	6/2003	State:	NI	Vehicle Out:
Color:	Int:	Condition:		Job #:		

TOTALS

Category	Basis		Rate	Cost $
Parts				510.34
Body Labor	1.7 hrs	@	$ 52.00 /hr	88.40
Paint Labor	5.1 hrs	@	$ 52.00 /hr	265.20
Paint Supplies	5.1 hrs	@	$ 30.00 /hr	153.00
Miscellaneous				20.00
Subtotal				1,036.94
Sales Tax	$ 1,036.94	@	4.1660 %	43.20
Grand Total				1,080.14

Exhibit 20

NITA CITY COLLISION CENTER

3156 INDUSTRIAL WAY, NITA CITY,
NITA 99992
Phone: (555) 246-4466
FAX: (555) 246-2132

Workfile ID:	8a394b19
Federal ID:	95-4536459
License Number:	RD-3307

Preliminary Estimate

Customer: BYRD, ROBERT

Written By: BRYAN OKINO

Insured: BYRD, ROBERT
Type of Loss:
Point of Impact: 12 Front

Policy #:
Date of Loss: April 20, 2012

Claim #:
Days to Repair: 0

Owner:
BYRD, ROBERT

(555) 346-9613 Cellular

Inspection Location:
NITA CITY COLLISION CENTER

3156 INDUSTRIAL WAY
NITA CITY
Repair Facility
(555) 246-4466 Business

Insurance Company:

VEHICLE

Year: 2010
Make: TOYO
Model: CAMRY LE
Color: GREY/1G3 Int:

Body Style: 4D SED
Engine: 4-2.5L-FI
Production Date: 12/2009
Condition:

VIN: 4T1BF3EK9AU098731
License: KZZ-031
State: NI
Job #:

Mileage In: 30506
Mileage Out:
Vehicle Out:

6 Speed Transmission	Console/Storage	Message Center	Power Windows
Air Conditioning	Cruise Control	Overdrive	Rear Defogger
Alarm	Driver Air Bag	Overhead Console	Search/Seek
AM Radio	Dual Mirrors	Passenger Air Bag	Stability Control
Anti-Lock Brakes (4)	FM Radio	Power Brakes	Steering Wheel Controls
Auxiliary Audio Connection	Front Side Impact Air Bags	Power Driver Seat	Stereo
Bucket Seats	Full Wheel Covers	Power Locks	Telescopic Wheel
CD Player	Head/Curtain Air Bags	Power Mirrors	Tilt Wheel
Clear Coat Paint	Intermittent Wipers	Power Steering	Tinted Glass
Cloth Seats	Keyless Entry	Power Trunk/Tailgate	Traction Control

National Institute for Trial Advocacy

Preliminary Estimate

Customer: BYRD, ROBERT

Vehicle: 2010 TOYO CAMRY LE 4D SED 4-2.5L-FI GREY/1G3

Line		Operation	Description	Qty	Extended Price $	Labor	Paint
1			FRONT BUMPER & GRILLE				
2		R&I	R&I bumper cover			1.4	
3	*	Rpr	Bumper cover US built w/o SE			1.0	2.6
4			Add for Clear Coat				1.0
5		R&I	RT Hole cover US built w/o XLE			0.1	
6		R&I	LT Hole cover US built w/o XLE			0.1	
7		R&I	Emblem US built			0.1	
8		R&I	License bracket			0.2	
9		R&I	R&I grille assy			0.3	
10	#	Refn	Color tint / color match				0.5
11	#	Rpr	Color sand and buff				0.4
12	#	Repl	Flex additive	1	10.00 T		
13	#	Subl	Hazardous waste removal	1	10.00 T		
			SUBTOTALS		20.00	3.2	4.5

ESTIMATE TOTALS

Category	Basis		Rate	Cost $
Parts				0.00
Body Labor	3.2 hrs	@	$ 52.00 /hr	166.40
Paint Labor	4.5 hrs	@	$ 52.00 /hr	234.00
Paint Supplies	4.5 hrs	@	$ 30.00 /hr	135.00
Body Supplies	1.0 hrs	@	$ 3.00 /hr	3.00
Miscellaneous				20.00
Subtotal				558.40
Sales Tax	$ 558.40	@	4.1660 %	23.26
Grand Total				581.66

FOR YOUR PROTECTION, NITA LAW REQUIRES YOU TO BE INFORMED THAT PRESENTING A FRAUDULENT CLAIM FOR PAYMENT OF A LOSS OR BENEFIT IS A CRIME PUNISHABLE BY FINES OR IMPRISONMENT, OR BOTH.

4/26/2012   024476   Page 2

National Institute for Trial Advocacy

Exhibit 21

Dr. David McCullough
Board Certified Doctor of Chiropractic Medicine
421 Central Avenue
Nita City, Nita 99993
555-461-2525

December 20, 2012

Kenneth Brown
5 Scott Place
Nita City Nita, 99994

Re: Invoice #9052

44 office visits at $125 per visit	$5,500
4% tax	$220
Total	$5,720

Exhibit 22

Dr. David McCullough
Board Certified Doctor of Chiropractic Medicine
421 Central Avenue,
Nita City, Nita 99993
555-461-2525

December 20, 2012

Harriet Cooperman
Nita City Tower, Suite 201
5 Main Street
Nita City, Nita 99992

Dear Ms. Cooperman:

In response to your request, I provide the following report about my care for your client, Kenneth Brown.

I have been Mr. Brown's health care provider for a back injury he received in an automobile accident in April of 2012. In reviewing his medical records from his internist, I note that he has been treated for various minor illnesses and provided annual physical examinations. He had no significant medical history or findings. He was a well-developed, well-nourished, male (6'4", 180 pounds) with a very active athletic background, including competitive tennis and swimming activities.

<u>HISTORY OF THIS INCIDENT</u>

On the morning of April 21, 2012, Patient telephoned his internist, Dr. Gomez, to request an emergency appointment that same day. Patient reported that on April 20, he was the driver of a car that had been rear-ended. Both vehicles sustained significant damage. At the moment of impact, Patient was leaning forward and looking to his left for possible approaching traffic, which made him more vulnerable to flexion-extension and torsion injury. Patient was wearing a combination lap and shoulder restraint, and the air bag did not deploy.

Patient said he was "shaken up" then, but had no meaningful pain or restricted motion for several hours. Patient did not seek any medical attention that day and traveled several hours by plane to a business meeting. As is typical, there was no immediate discomfort to patient after collision. He became very uncomfortable that night and decided to come home to seek medical assistance the next morning, at which point, again as is typical, he was in quite a lot of pain.

At the time of Patient's first office visit to internist, Patient complained of a headache, severe pain in neck, and moderate pain in lower back. Upon examination, 40 percent restriction of neck rotation and flexion and 30 percent limitation of low back flexion on straight leg raising (more on the left than the right) was noted. There was point tenderness and muscle spasm at or near C-6 and C-7 and at or near L-4 and L-5. A routine neurological examination was otherwise within normal limits with negative Babinski and Romberg tests, and bilaterally active and equal reflexes at the elbow, wrist, knee, and ankle. MRIs ordered, negative for herniation. Degeneration noted at L4-L5. Otherwise normal. Rest and ibuprofen for pain prescribed. Follow-up evaluation in ten days.

<u>TREATMENT</u>

Patient was first seen on April 23, 2012. Complete examination and chiropractic adjustment given. Progressive course of physical therapy recommended increasing from twice per week to three times per week over three months. Chiropractic adjustment schedule agreed upon. 3X/week until improvement. Confirmed diagnosis of Dr. Gomez. Burmeister's Physical Therapy Clinic later reported that Mr. Brown appeared for thirty physical therapy treatments there between May 5 and August 20, 2012, which included deep heat, hot baths, massage, aqua therapy, and cervical traction.

When he returned to my office on May 1, 2012, his condition had not improved. He had essentially the same complaints, and my findings were substantially the same. I began a regimen of Flexeril 10 mg. t.i.d. as a muscle relaxant, and Percocet 10 mg. p.r.n. for pain. I cautioned him that alcoholic beverages are contraindicated and potentially harmful while he uses these medications.

At my direction, he returned for forty-two further office visits, the most recent of which was last week on December 16. In July I prescribed a CT-scan of his neck and back at Nita City Hospital, which the radiologist there interpreted as within normal limits. In August, I referred Mr. Brown to Dr. Phileas Fogg, a board certified orthopedist, who reported essentially the same findings I had made and ruled out a herniated nucleuous pulposus in the neck or back.

<u>OPINION</u>

Mr. Brown suffered a flexion-extension myofascial injury to his neck and low back, which produced moderate disability for at least three months and some continued disability thereafter. In my opinion, he will probably suffer some continued pain and disability indefinitely on extremes of motion, which might limit or preclude his participation in active athletic efforts. He has worked on stretching exercises and intends to try to play tennis. He has reported missing a number of days from his employment in the early course of his treatment. He may miss some days hereafter during normal exacerbations of his symptoms. He is to return to my office for further evaluation and adjustment as needed. I would expect Mr. Brown to continue such treatments for at least the next six to eight months.

My office manager advises me that my professional fees for treating this patient's injury have been $5,720, including tax. At your request, I reviewed Mr. Brown's bills from Burmeister's Clinic ($1,450.00), Nita City Hospital for CT-scan ($400.00), Nita City Radiologists, Inc. ($150.00), and Dr. Fogg ($125.00). I found them all to be reasonable charges for necessary medical care. Please contact me if you require any further information.

Please remit $350.00 as my charge for this report.

Very truly yours,

David Mc Cullough

Dr. David McCullough

Special Impeachment Problems

PROBLEM 1

On direct examination, the plaintiff has testified to the following: "I stopped before I got to the cross-walk. My car wasn't in the crosswalk until after he smashed into me."

For the defendant, conduct the impeachment of Brown.

Option A: Conduct the impeachment of Brown using whatever portions you choose of the transcript of his testimony that appears in this volume.

Option B: Conduct the impeachment of Brown using whatever portions you choose of the video recording of his deposition testimony that appears in the PowerPoint slide show.

Option C: Conduct the impeachment of Brown using whatever portions you choose of the video recording of his deposition testimony with the scrolling written transcript appearing beneath it that appears in the PowerPoint slide show.

PROBLEM 2

On direct examination, the defendant has testified to the following: "At the time of the accident, I was headed for an appointment at Ferguson Auto Body. I was going slowly. I wasn't in any rush."

For plaintiff, conduct the impeachment of Byrd.

Thumbnails of PowerPoint Slides

Blank Slide   Slide 1

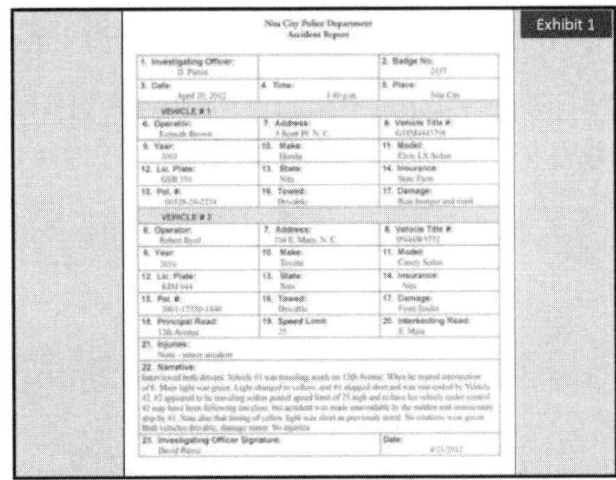

Exhibit 1   Slide 2

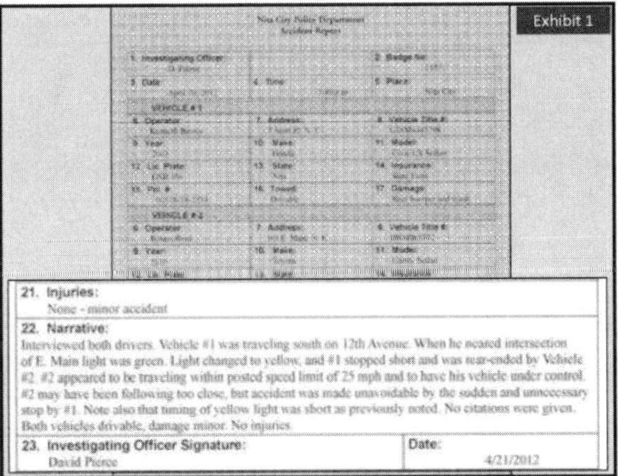

21. Injuries:
    None - minor accident
22. Narrative:
Interviewed both drivers. Vehicle #1 was traveling south on 12th Avenue. When he neared intersection of E. Main light was green. Light changed to yellow, and #1 stopped short and was rear-ended by Vehicle #2. #2 appeared to be traveling within posted speed limit of 25 mph and to have his vehicle under control. #2 may have been following too close, but accident was made unavoidable by the sudden and unnecessary stop by #1. Note also that timing of yellow light was short as previously noted. No citations were given. Both vehicles drivable, damage minor. No injuries.
23. Investigating Officer Signature: Date:
    David Pierce   4/21/2012

Exhibit 1   Slide 3

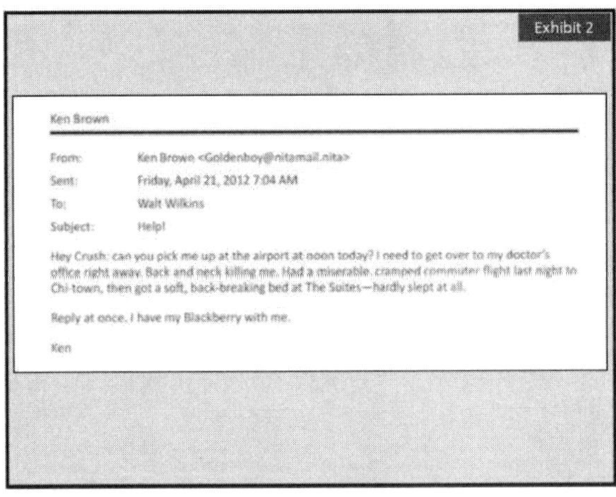

Ken Brown

From: Ken Brown <Goldenboy@nitamail.nita>
Sent: Friday, April 21, 2012 7:04 AM
To: Walt Wilkins
Subject: Help!

Hey Crush: can you pick me up at the airport at noon today? I need to get over to my doctor's office right away. Back and neck killing me. Had a miserable, cramped commuter flight last night to Chi-town, then got a soft, back-breaking bed at The Suites—hardly slept at all.

Reply at once. I have my Blackberry with me.

Ken

Exhibit 2   Slide 4

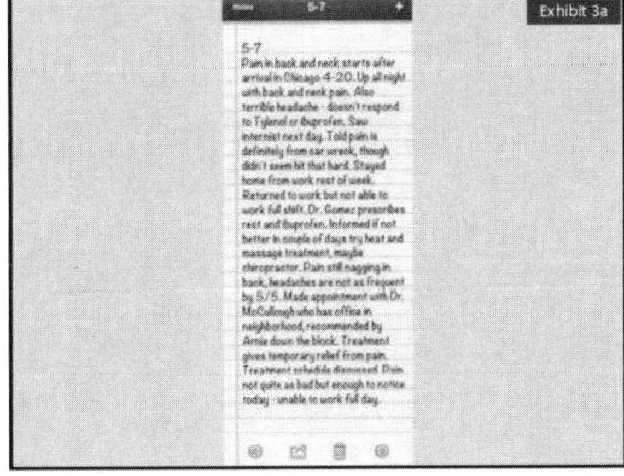

5-7
Pain in back and neck starts after arrival in Chicago 4-20. Up all night with back and neck pain. Also terrible headache - doesn't respond to Tylenol or ibuprofen. Saw internist next day. Told pain is definitely from car wreck, though didn't seem hit that hard. Stayed home from work rest of week. Returned to work but not able to work full shift. Dr. Gomez prescribes rest and ibuprofen. Informed if not better in couple of days try heat and massage treatment, maybe chiropractor. Pain still nagging in back, headaches are not as frequent by 5/5. Made appointment with Dr. McCullough who has office in neighborhood, recommended by Arnie down the block. Treatment gives temporary relief from pain. Treatment schedule discussed. Pain not quite as bad but enough to notice today - unable to work full day.

Exhibit 3a   Slide 5

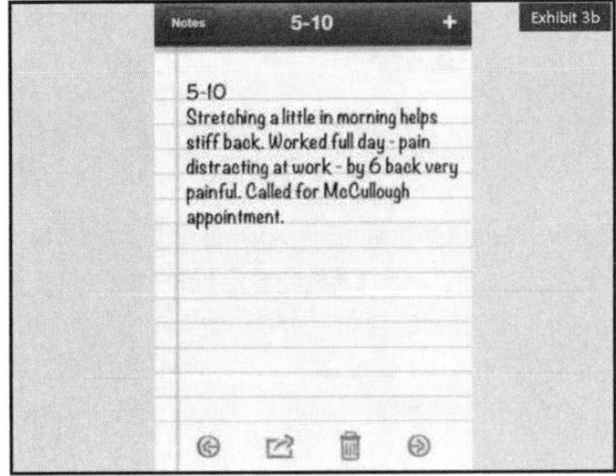

5-10
Stretching a little in morning helps stiff back. Worked full day - pain distracting at work - by 6 back very painful. Called for McCullough appointment.

Exhibit 3b   Slide 6

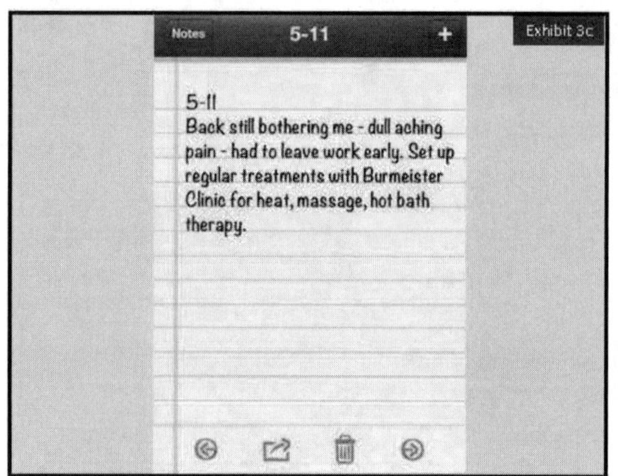

Exhibit 3c

Slide 7

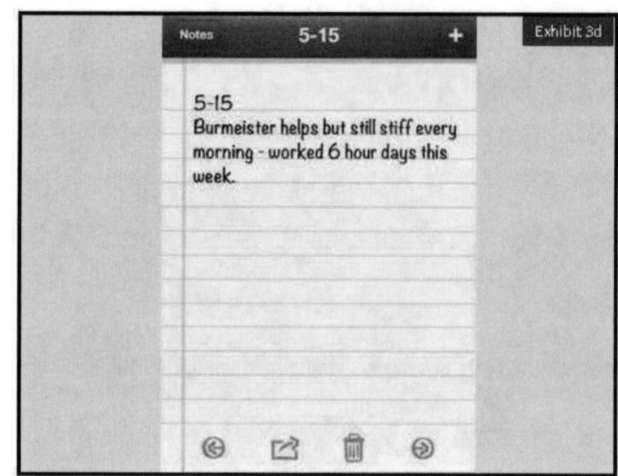

Exhibit 3d

Slide 8

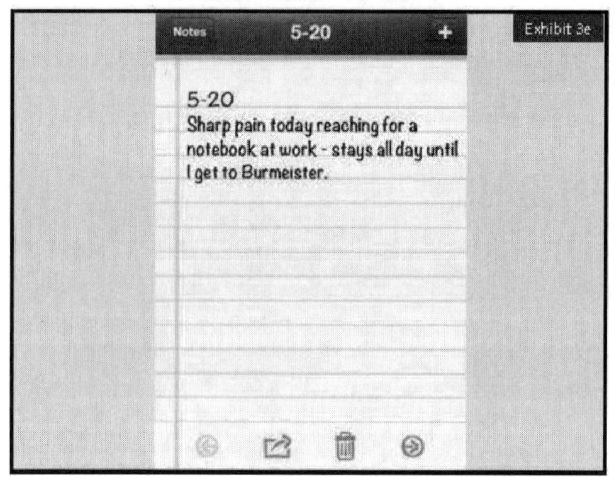

Exhibit 3e

Slide 9

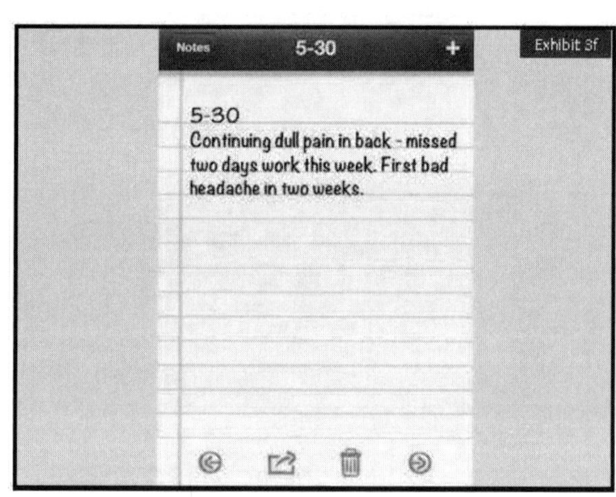

Exhibit 3f

Slide 10

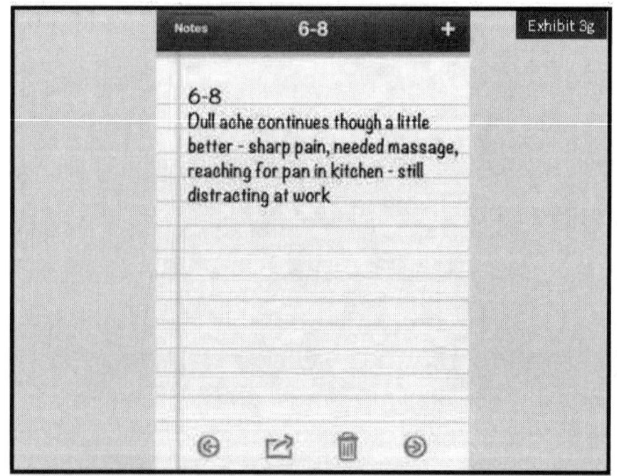

Exhibit 3g

Slide 11

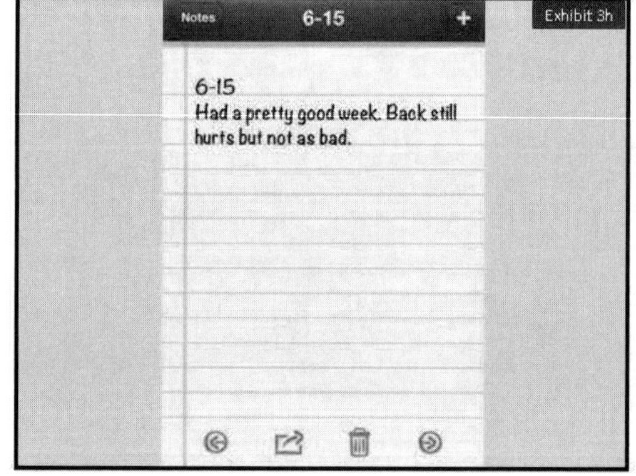

Exhibit 3h

Slide 12

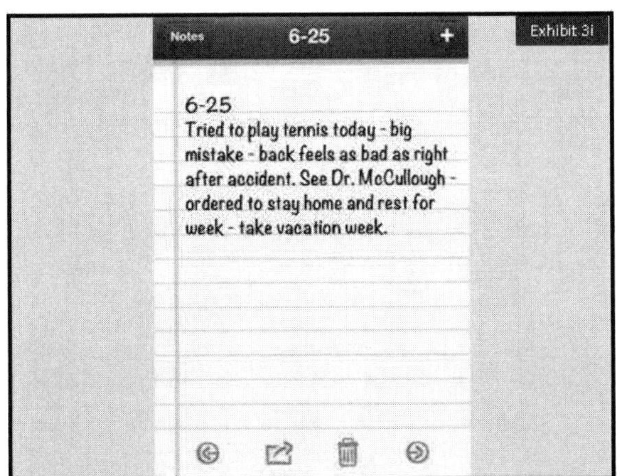

Exhibit 3i   Slide 13

Exhibit 3j   Slide 14

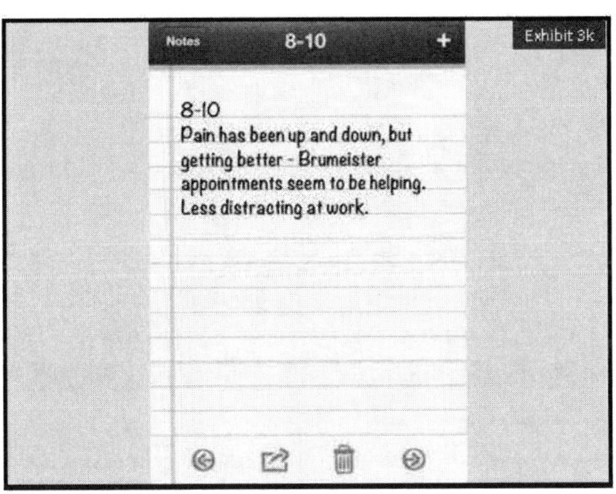

Exhibit 3k   Slide 15

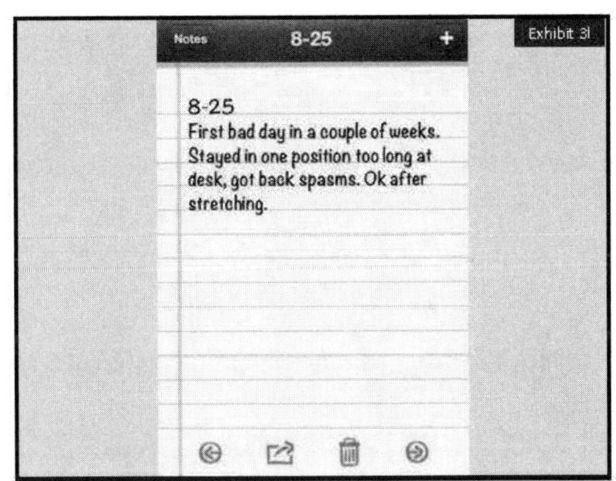

Exhibit 3l   Slide 16

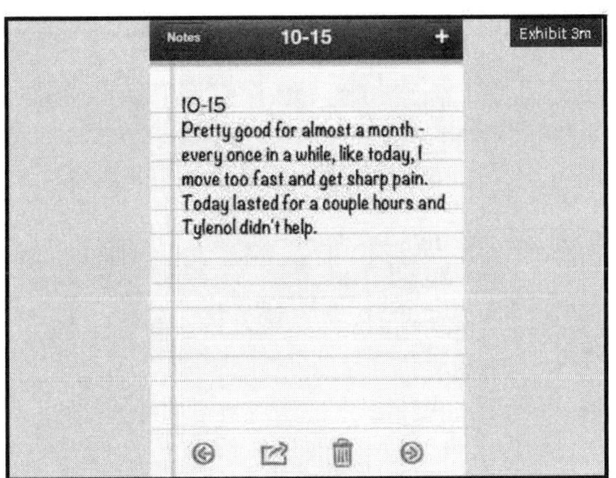

Exhibit 3m   Slide 17

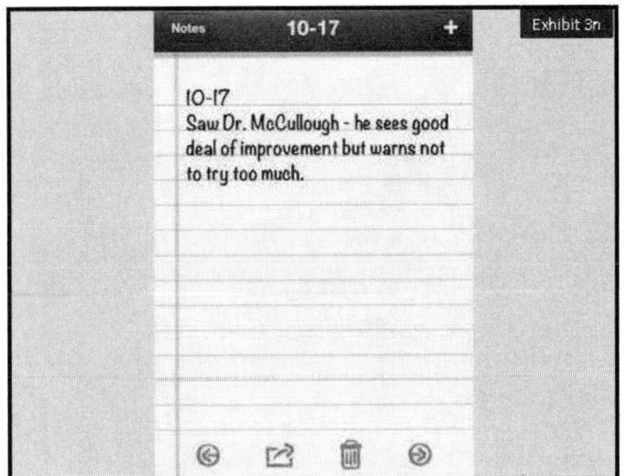

Exhibit 3n   Slide 18

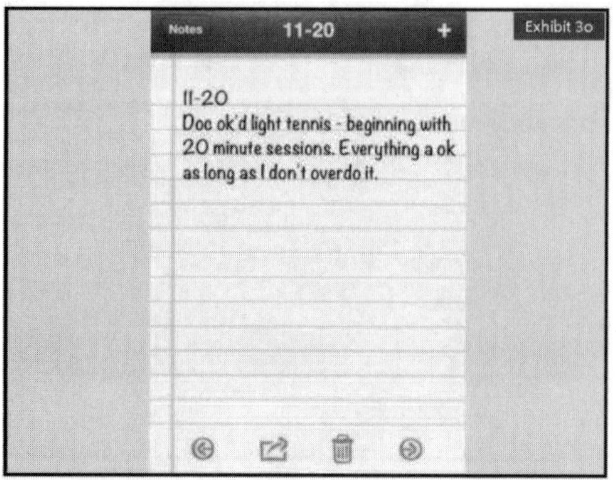

Exhibit 3o — Slide 19

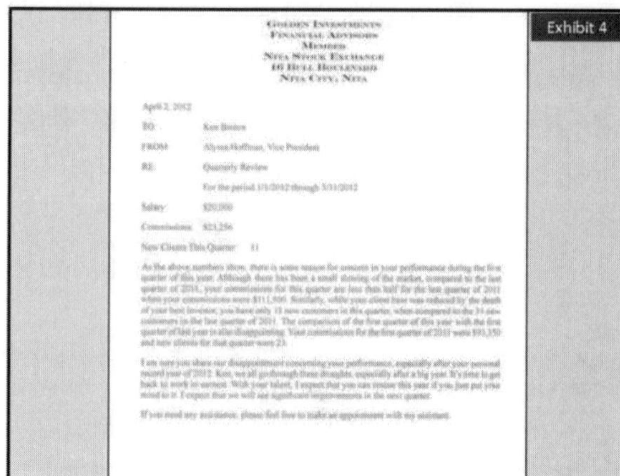

Exhibit 4 — Slide 20

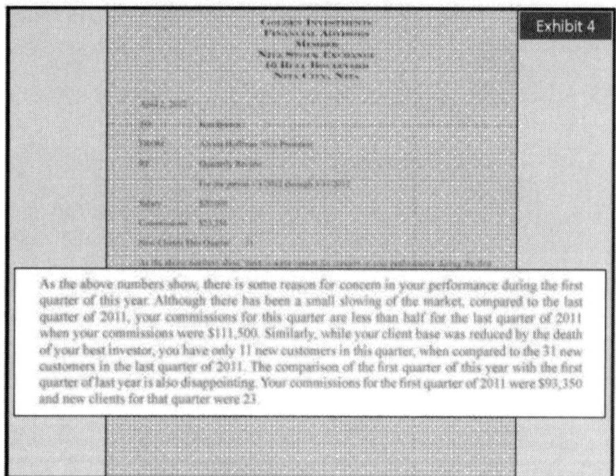

Exhibit 4 — Slide 21

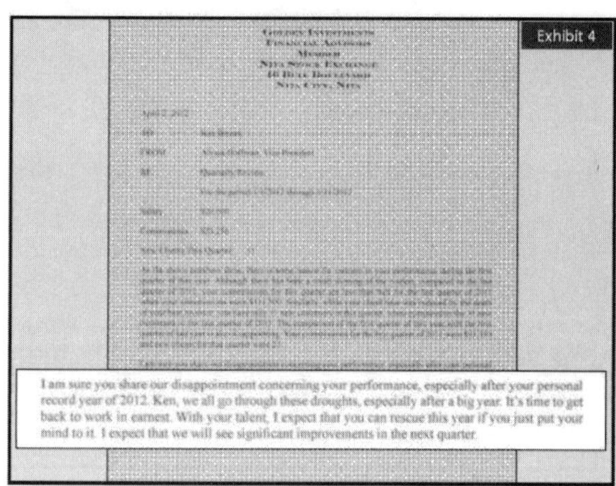

Exhibit 4 — Slide 22

Exhibit 5 — Slide 23

Exhibit 6 — Slide 24

Exhibit 7   Slide 25

Exhibit 8   Slide 26

Exhibit 9   Slide 27

Exhibit 10   Slide 28

Exhibit 11   Slide 29

Exhibit 12   Slide 30

Two Months Later   Slide 31

Two Months Later   Slide 32

Two Months Later   Slide 33

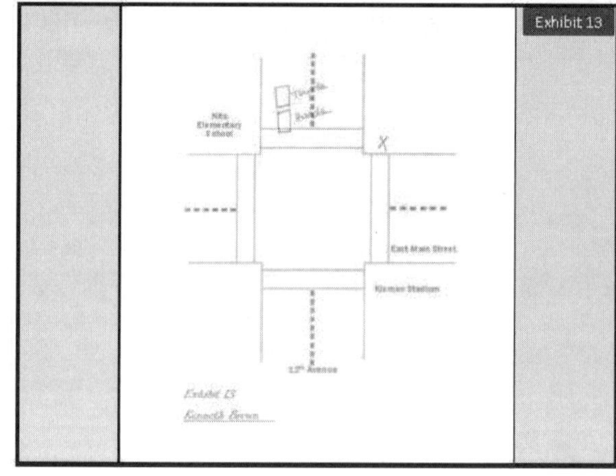

Exhibit 13   Slide 34

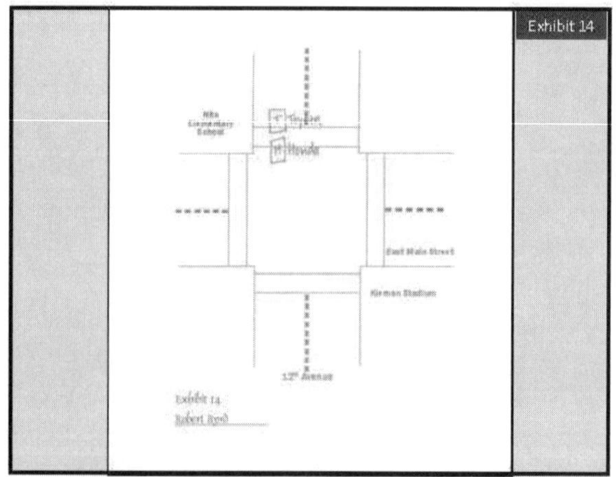

Exhibit 14   Slide 35

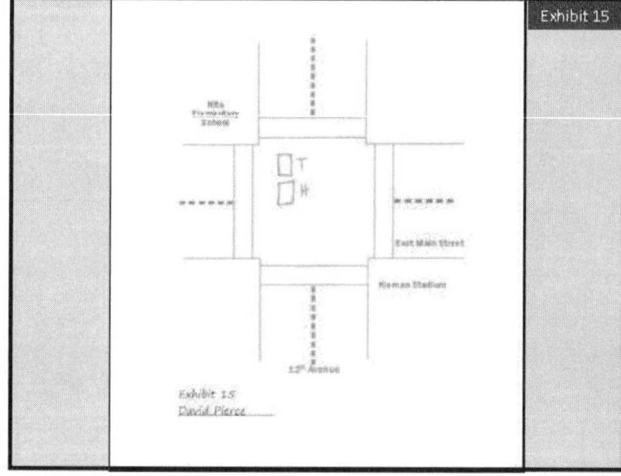

Exhibit 15   Slide 36

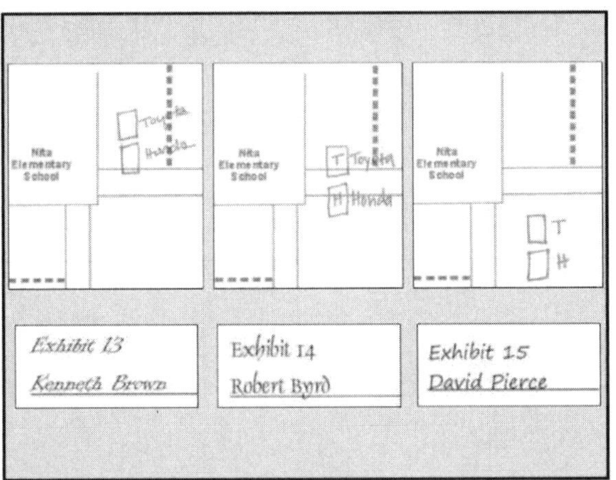

Exhibit 13, 14, & 15   Slide 37

Exhibit 16   Slide 38

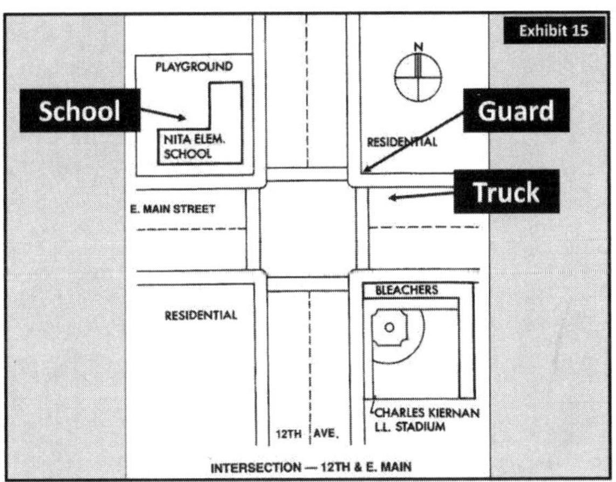

Exhibit 16   Slide 39

Exhibit 17   Slide 40

Exhibit 18   Slide 41

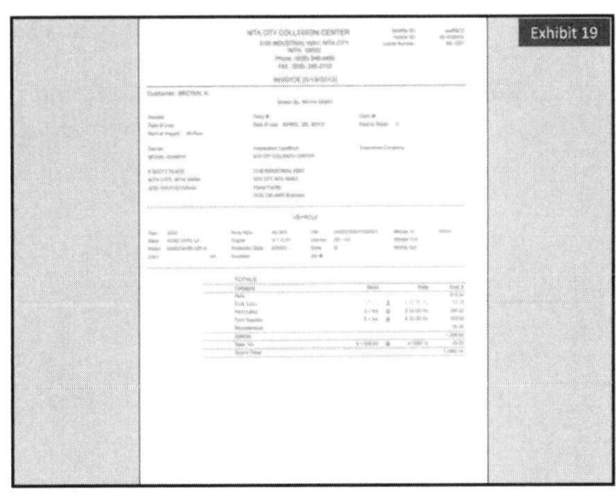

Exhibit 19   Slide 42

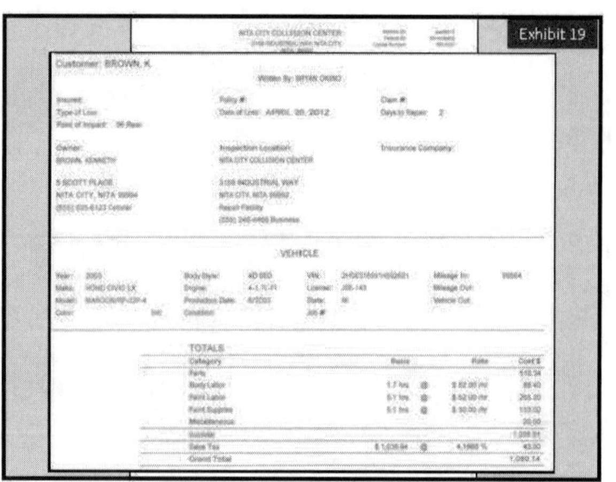

Exhibit 19   Slide 43

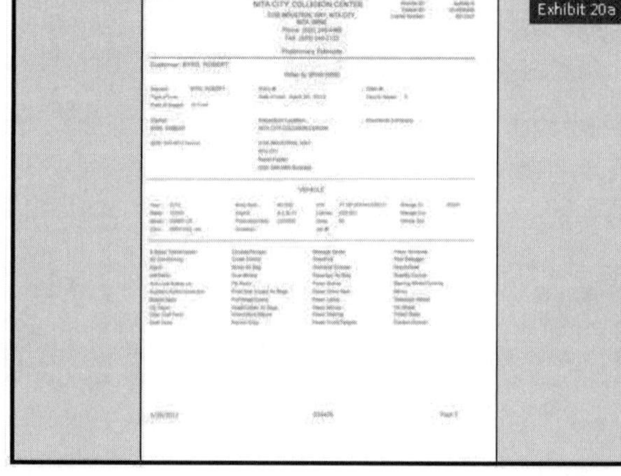

Exhibit 20a   Slide 44

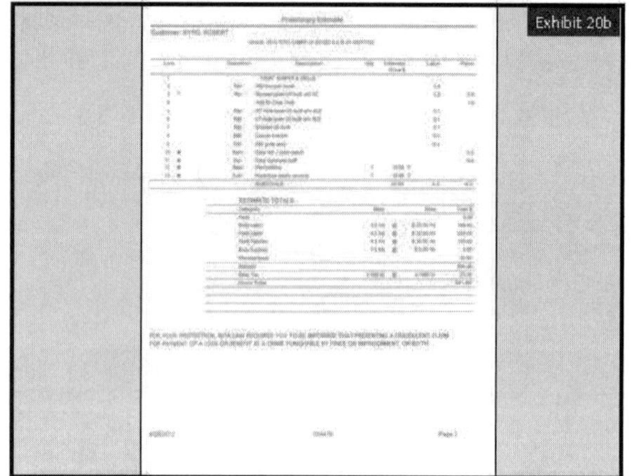

Exhibit 20b   Slide 45

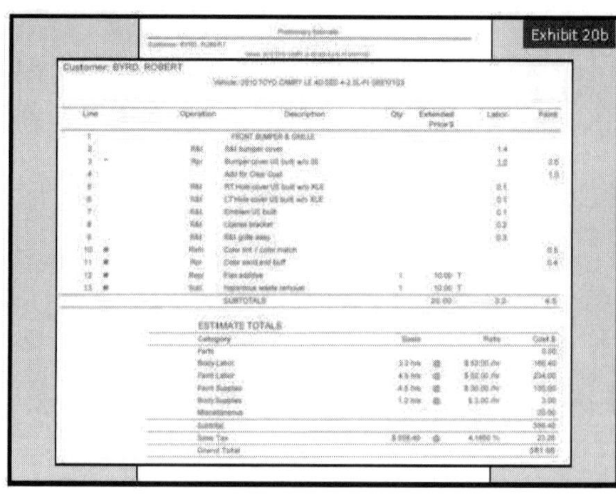

Exhibit 20b   Slide 46

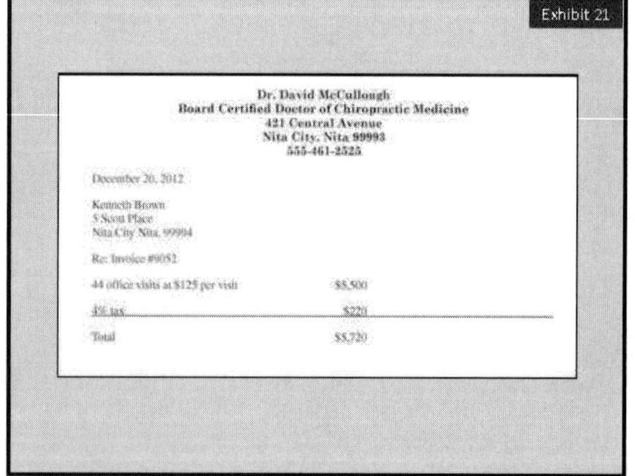

Exhibit 21   Slide 47

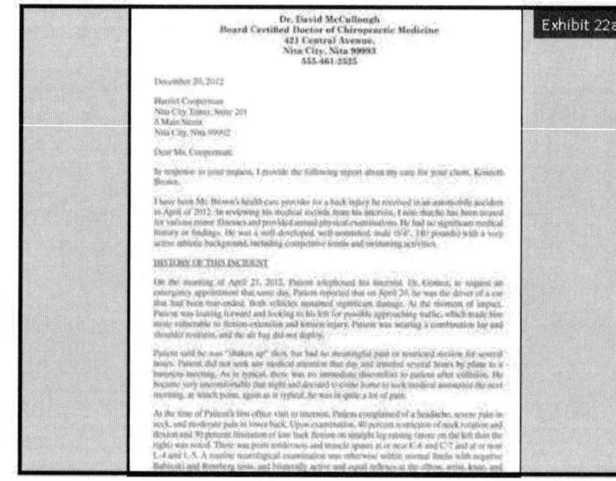

Exhibit 22a   Slide 48

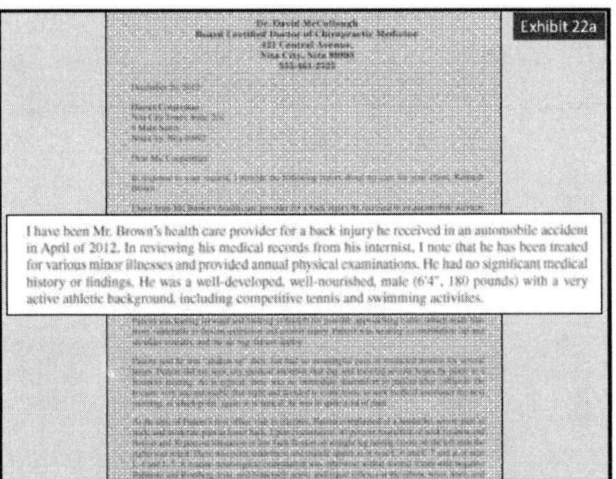

I have been Mr. Brown's health care provider for a back injury he received in an automobile accident in April of 2012. In reviewing his medical records from his internist, I note that he has been treated for various minor illnesses and provided annual physical examinations. He had no significant medical history or findings. He was a well-developed, well-nourished, male (6'4", 180 pounds) with a very active athletic background, including competitive tennis and swimming activities.

Exhibit 22a — Slide 49

On the morning of April 21, 2012, Patient telephoned his internist, Dr. Gomez, to request an emergency appointment that same day. Patient reported that on April 20, he was the driver of a car that had been rear-ended. Both vehicles sustained significant damage. At the moment of impact, Patient was leaning forward and looking to his left for possible approaching traffic, which made him more vulnerable to flexion-extension and torsion injury. Patient was wearing a combination lap and shoulder restraint, and the air bag did not deploy.

Exhibit 22a — Slide 50

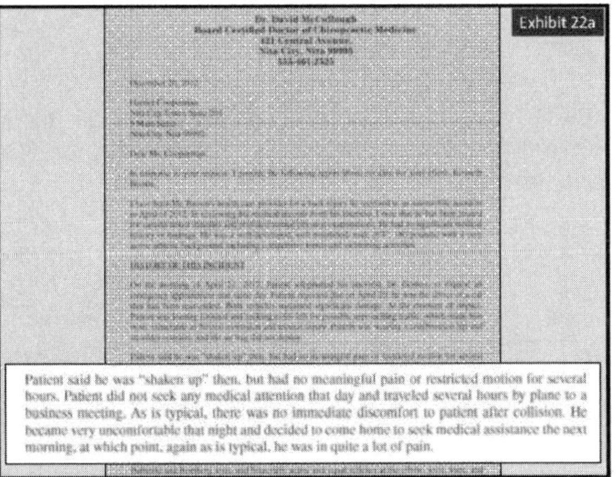

Patient said he was "shaken up" then, but had no meaningful pain or restricted motion for several hours. Patient did not seek any medical attention that day and traveled several hours by plane to a business meeting. As is typical, there was no immediate discomfort to patient after collision. He became very uncomfortable that night and decided to come home to seek medical assistance the next morning, at which point, again as is typical, he was in quite a lot of pain.

Exhibit 22a — Slide 51

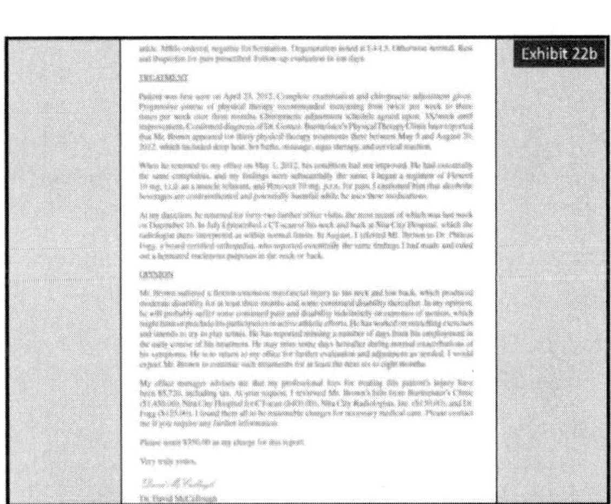

artic. MRIs ordered, negative for herniation. Degeneration noted at L4-L5. Otherwise normal. Rest and Ibuprofen for pain prescribed. Follow-up evaluation in ten days.

TREATMENT

Patient was first seen on April 23, 2012. Complete examination and chiropractic adjustment given. Progressive course of physical therapy recommended increasing from twice per week to three times per week over three months. Chiropractic adjustment schedule agreed upon. 3X/week until improvement. Confirmed diagnosis of Dr. Gomez. Burmeister's Physical Therapy Clinic later reported that Mr. Brown appeared for thirty physical therapy treatments there between May 5 and August 20, 2012, which included deep heat, hot baths, massage, aqua therapy, and cervical traction.

When he returned to my office on May 1, 2012, his condition had not improved. He had essentially the same complaints, and my findings were substantially the same. I began a regimen of Flexeril 10 mg. t.i.d. as a muscle relaxant, and Percocet 10 mg. p.r.n. for pain. I cautioned him that alcoholic beverages are contraindicated and potentially harmful while he uses these medications.

At my direction, he returned for forty-two further office visits, the most recent of which was last week on December 16. In July I prescribed a CT-scan of his neck and back at Nita City Hospital, which the radiologist there interpreted as within normal limits. In August, I referred Mr. Brown to Dr. Phileas Fogg, a board certified orthopedist, who reported essentially the same findings I had made and ruled out a herniated nucleous pulposus in the neck or back.

OPINION

Mr. Brown suffered a flexion-extension myofascial injury to his neck and low back, which produced moderate disability for at least three months and some continued disability thereafter. In my opinion, he will probably suffer some continued pain and disability indefinitely on extremes of motion, which might limit or preclude his participation in active athletic efforts. He has worked on stretching exercises and intends to try to play tennis. He has reported missing a number of days from his employment in the early course of his treatment. He may miss some days hereafter during normal exacerbations of his symptoms. He is to return to my office for further evaluation and adjustment as needed. I would expect Mr. Brown to continue such treatments for at least the next six to eight months.

Very truly yours,

Dr. David McCullough

Exhibit 22b — Slide 52

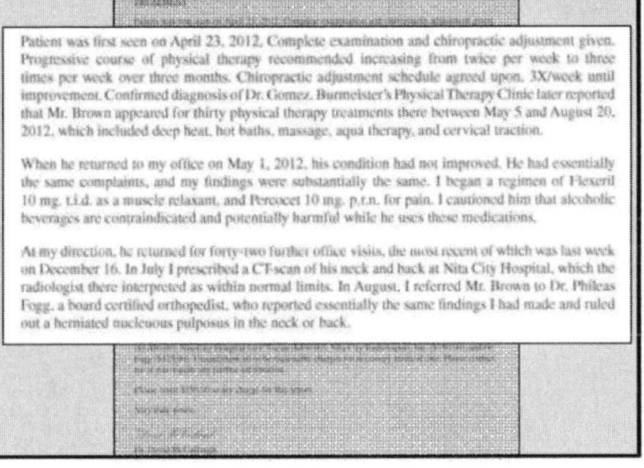

Patient was first seen on April 23, 2012. Complete examination and chiropractic adjustment given. Progressive course of physical therapy recommended increasing from twice per week to three times per week over three months. Chiropractic adjustment schedule agreed upon. 3X/week until improvement. Confirmed diagnosis of Dr. Gomez. Burmeister's Physical Therapy Clinic later reported that Mr. Brown appeared for thirty physical therapy treatments there between May 5 and August 20, 2012, which included deep heat, hot baths, massage, aqua therapy, and cervical traction.

When he returned to my office on May 1, 2012, his condition had not improved. He had essentially the same complaints, and my findings were substantially the same. I began a regimen of Flexeril 10 mg. t.i.d. as a muscle relaxant, and Percocet 10 mg. p.r.n. for pain. I cautioned him that alcoholic beverages are contraindicated and potentially harmful while he uses these medications.

At my direction, he returned for forty-two further office visits, the most recent of which was last week on December 16. In July I prescribed a CT-scan of his neck and back at Nita City Hospital, which the radiologist there interpreted as within normal limits. In August, I referred Mr. Brown to Dr. Phileas Fogg, a board certified orthopedist, who reported essentially the same findings I had made and ruled out a herniated nucleous pulposus in the neck or back.

Exhibit 22b — Slide 53

Mr. Brown suffered a flexion-extension myofascial injury to his neck and low back, which produced moderate disability for at least three months and some continued disability thereafter. In my opinion, he will probably suffer some continued pain and disability indefinitely on extremes of motion, which might limit or preclude his participation in active athletic efforts. He has worked on stretching exercises and intends to try to play tennis. He has reported missing a number of days from his employment in the early course of his treatment. He may miss some days hereafter during normal exacerbations of his symptoms. He is to return to my office for further evaluation and adjustment as needed. I would expect Mr. Brown to continue such treatments for at least the next six to eight months.

Exhibit 22b — Slide 54

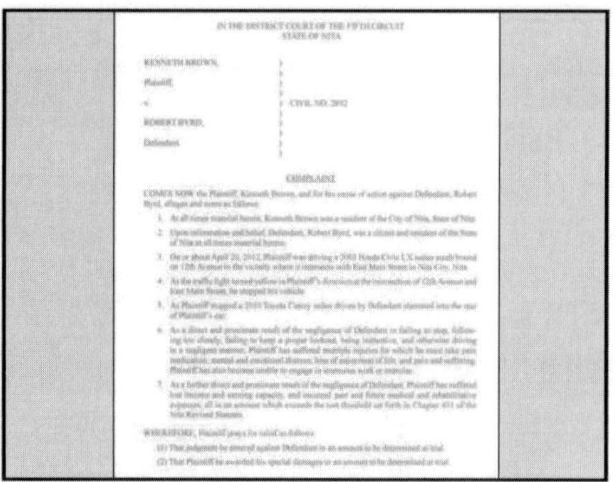

Complaint, p. 1   Slide 55

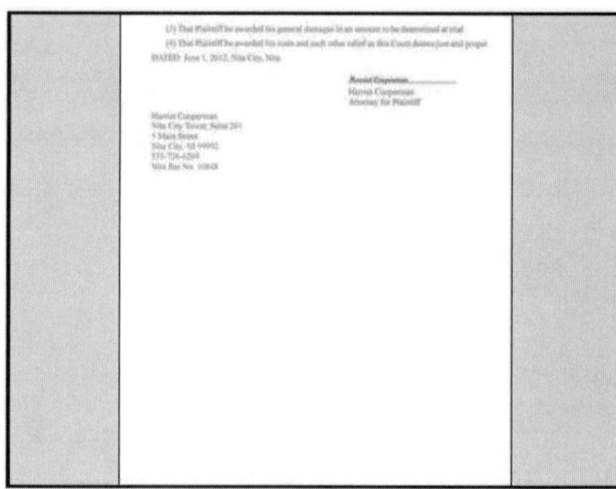

Complaint, p. 2   Slide 56

Jury Instructions   Slide 57

Jury Instruction 3   Slide 58

Jury Instruction 4   Slide 59

Jury Instruction 5   Slide 60

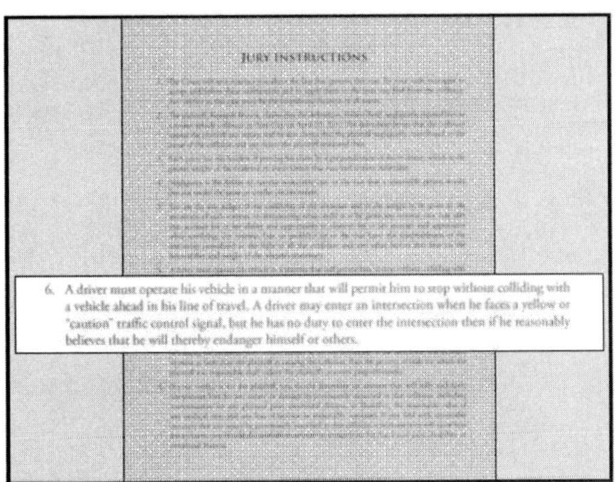

Jury Instruction 6   Slide 61

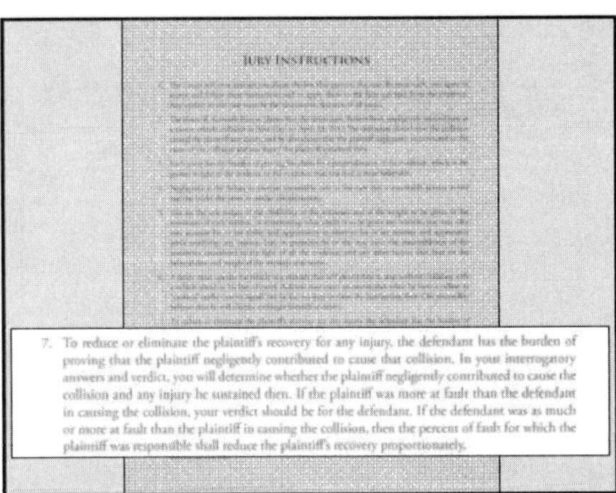

Jury Instruction 7   Slide 62

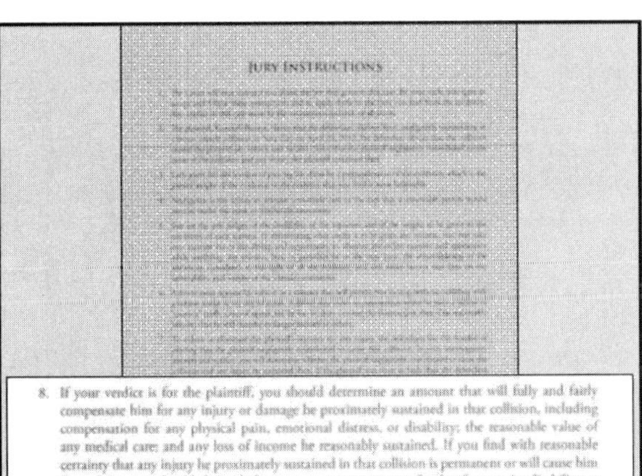

Jury Instruction 8   Slide 63

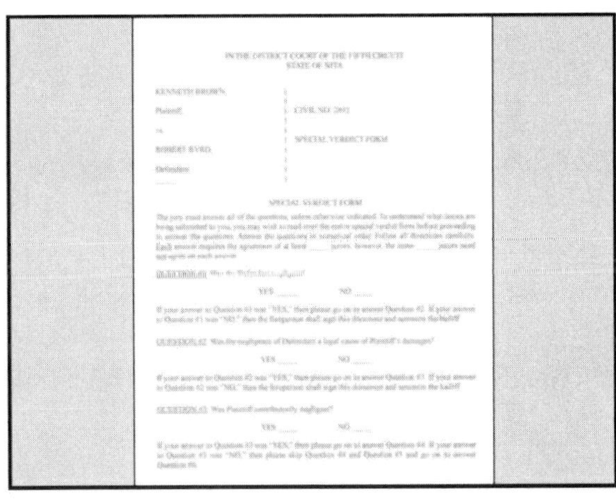

Special Verdict Form, p. 1   Slide 64

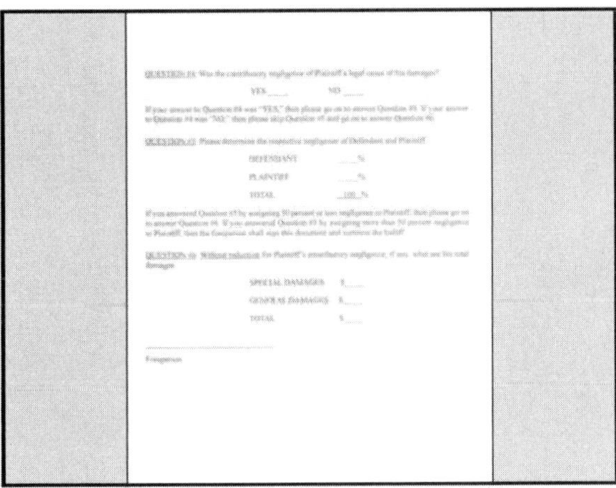

Special Verdict Form, p. 2   Slide 65

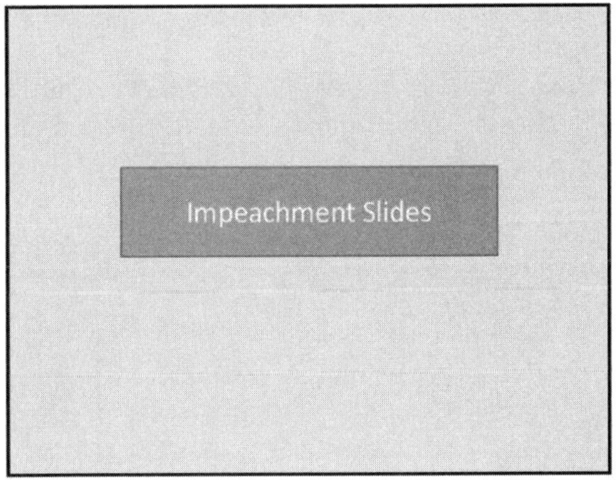

Impeachment Slides   Slide 66

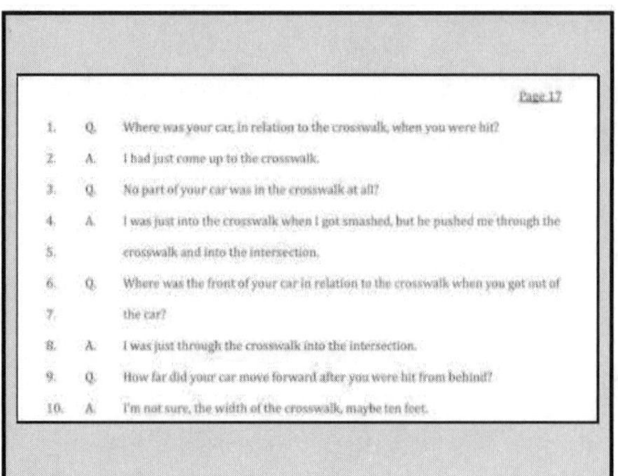

Brown Transcript p. 17, 1-10   Slide 67

Brown Video p. 17, 1-10   Slide 68

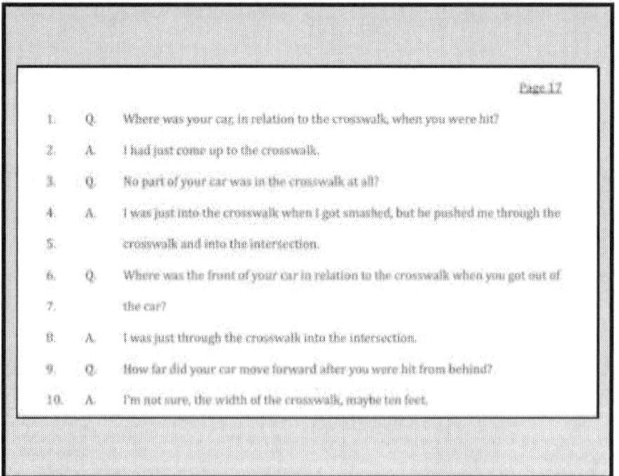

Brown Q & A Reveal p. 17, 1-10   Slide 69

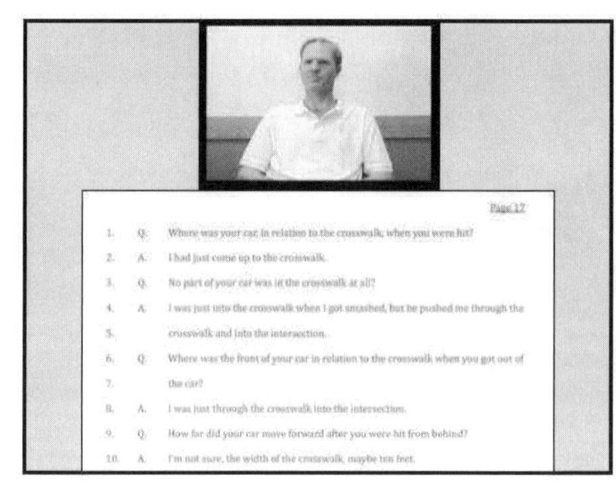

Brown Q & A Reveal p. 17, 1-10   Slide 70

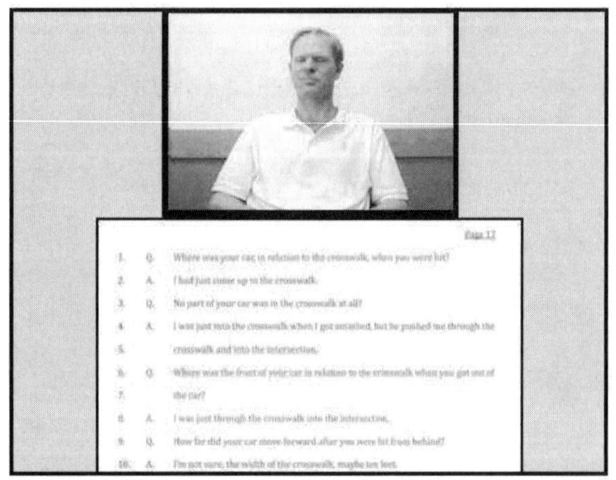

Brown Video & Tr. p.17, 1-10   Slide 71

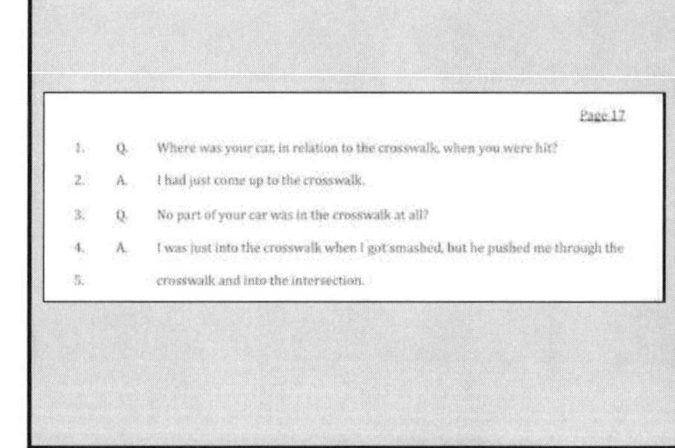

Brown Transcript p. 17, 1-5   Slide 72

Brown Video p. 17, 1-5   Slide 73

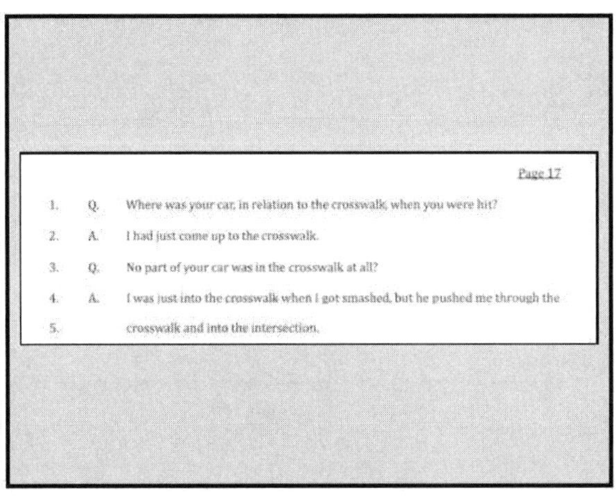

Brown Q & A Reveal p. 17, 1-5   Slide 74

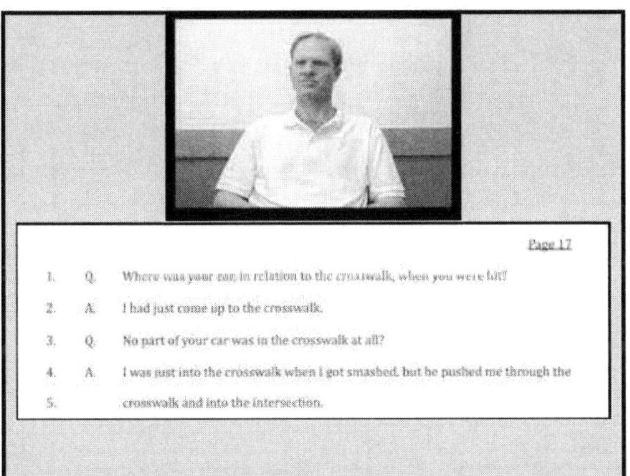

Brown Q & A Reveal p. 17, 1-5   Slide 75

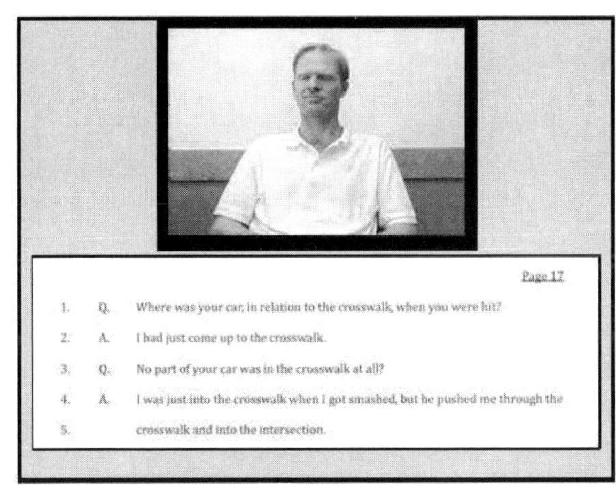

Brown Video & Tr. p. 17, 1-5   Slide 76

Brown Transcript p. 49, 1-16   Slide 77

Brown Video p. 49, 1-16   Slide 78

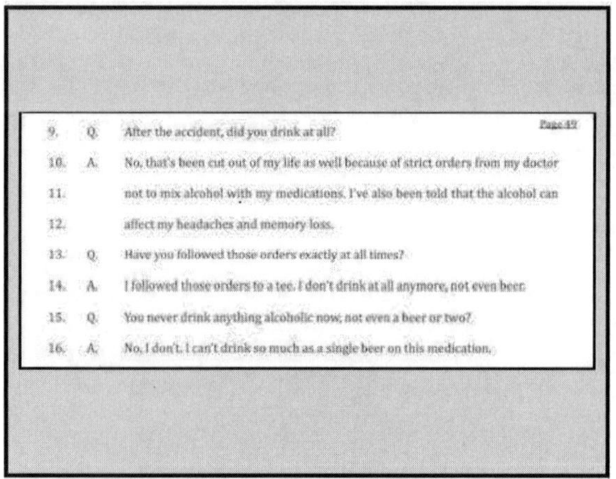

Brown Transcript p. 49, 9-16   Slide 79

Brown Video p. 49, 9-16   Slide 80

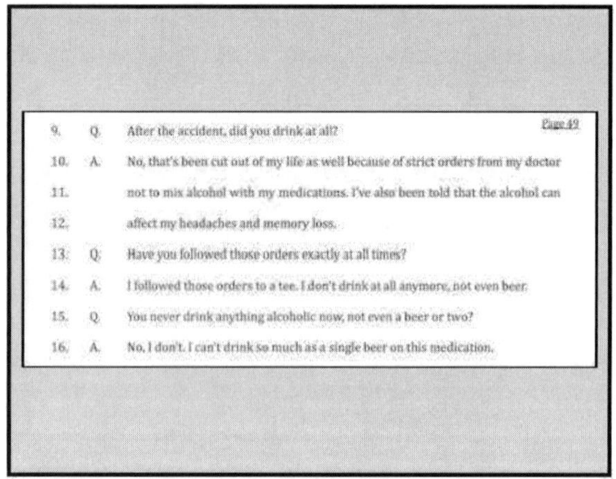

Brown Q & A Reveal p. 49, 9-16   Slide 81

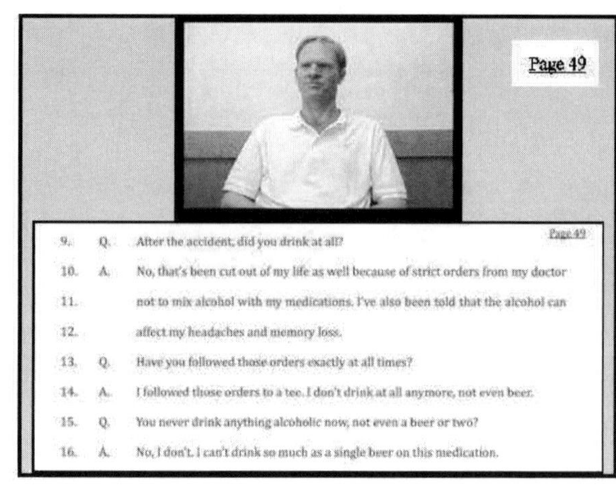

Brown Q & A Reveal p. 49, 9-16   Slide 82

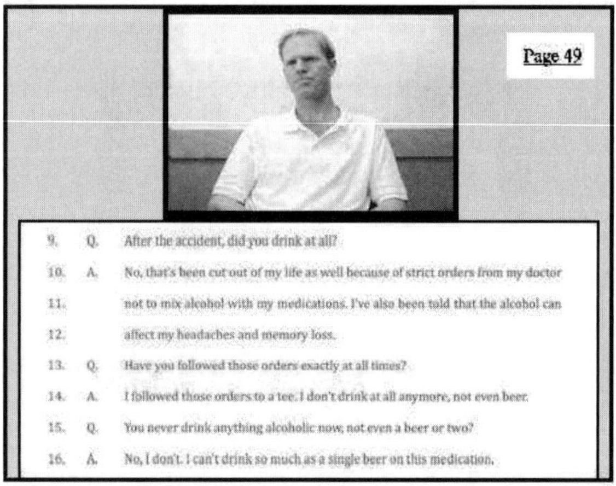

Brown Video & Tr. p. 49, 9-16   Slide 83

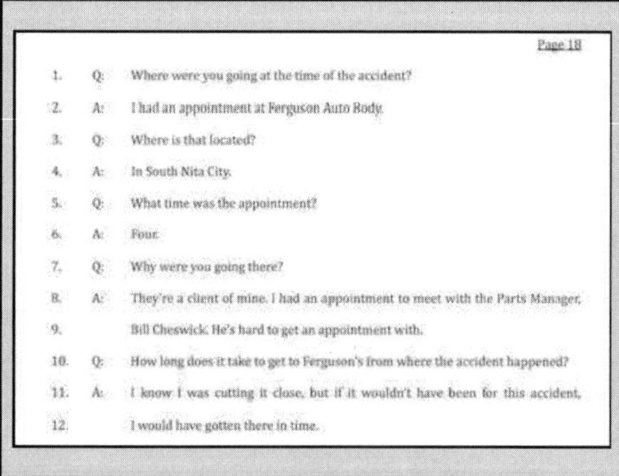

Byrd Transcript p. 18, 1-12   Slide 84

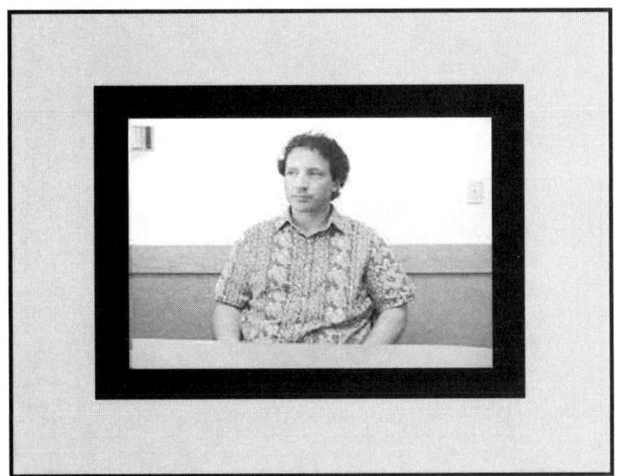

Byrd Video p. 18, 1-12   Slide 85

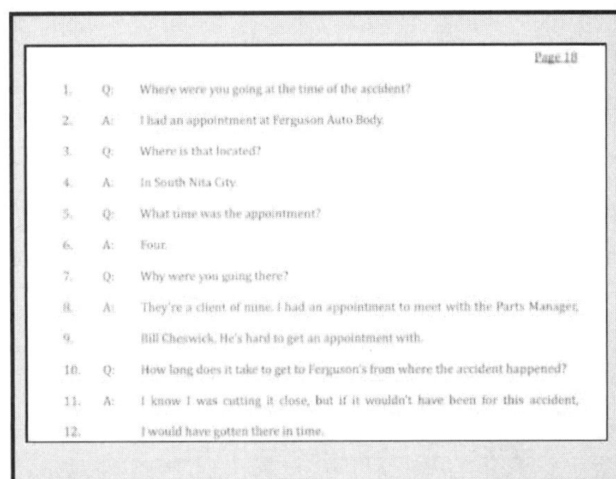

Byrd Q & A Reveal p. 18, 1-12   Slide 86

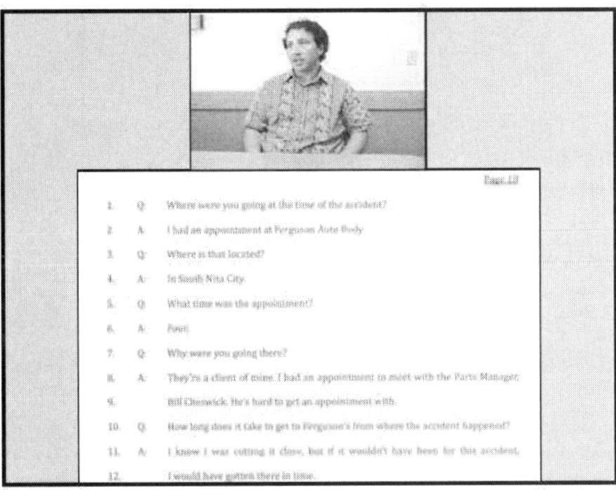

Byrd Q & A Reveal p. 18, 1-12   Slide 87

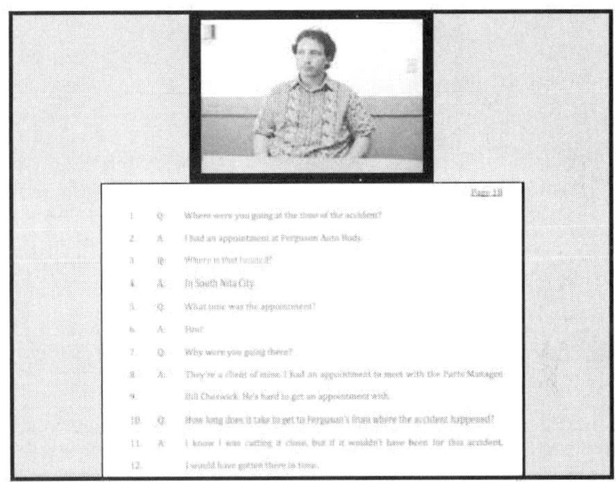

Byrd Video & Tr. p. 18, 1-12   Slide 88

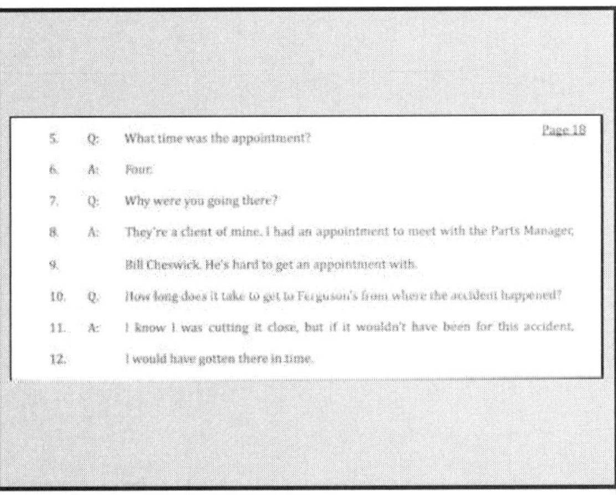

Byrd Transcript p. 18, 5-12   Slide 89

Byrd Video p. 18, 5-12   Slide 90

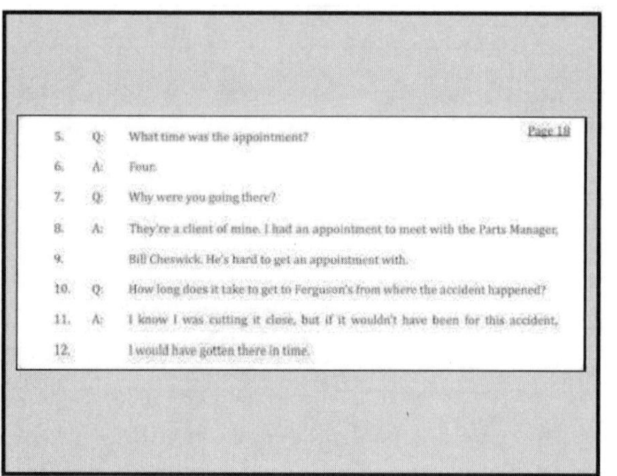

Byrd Q & A Reveal p. 18, 5-12   Slide 91

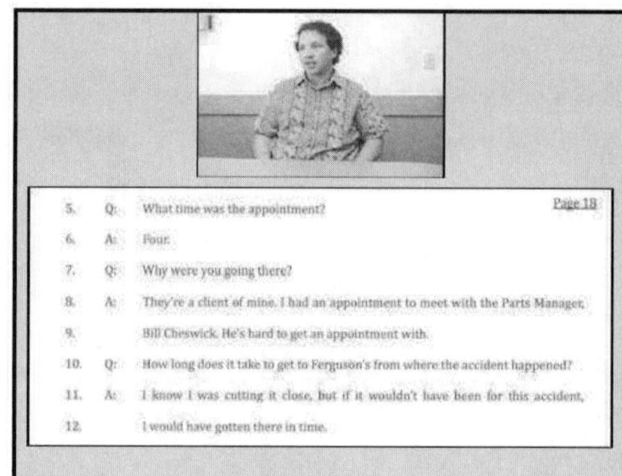

Byrd Q & A Reveal p. 18, 5-12   Slide 92

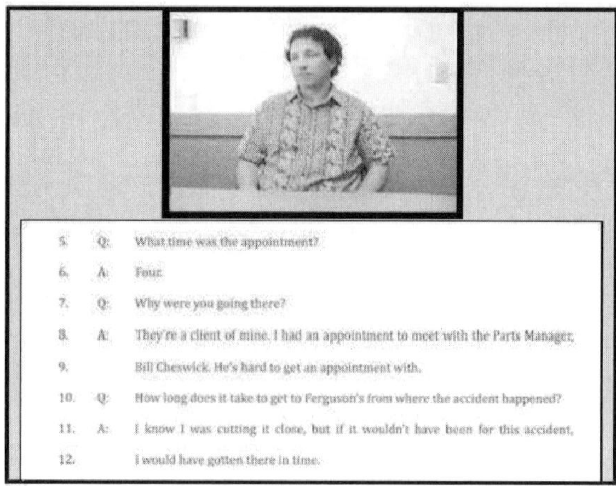

Byrd Video & Tr. p. 18, 5-12   Slide 93

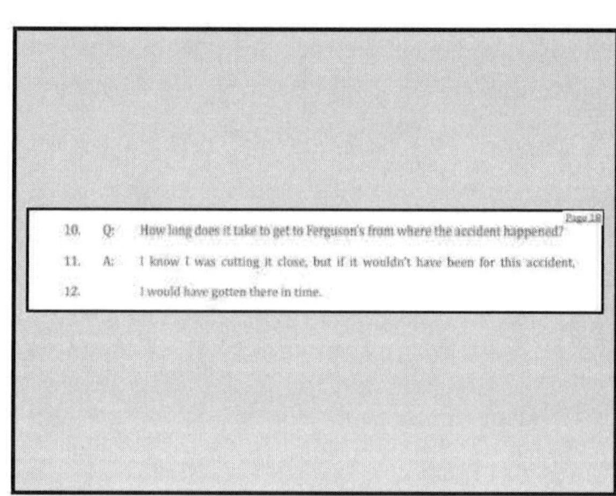

Byrd Transcript p. 18, 10-12   Slide 94

Byrd Video p. 18, 10-12   Slide 95

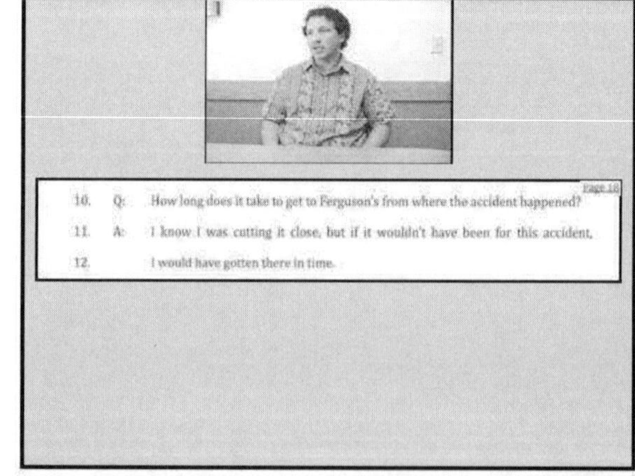

Byrd Q & A Reveal p. 18, 10-12   Slide 96

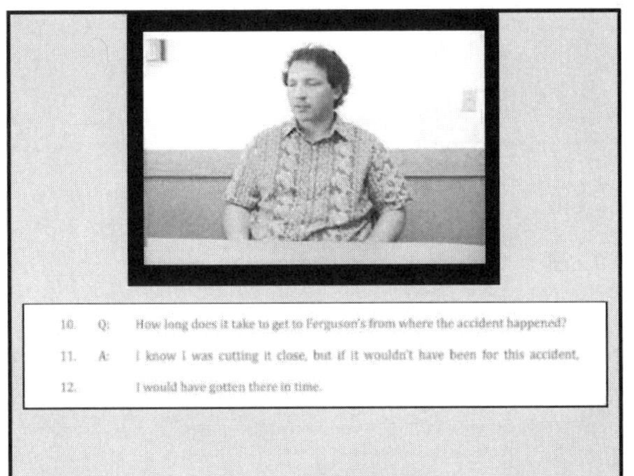

Byrd Q & A Reveal p. 18, 10-12   Slide 97

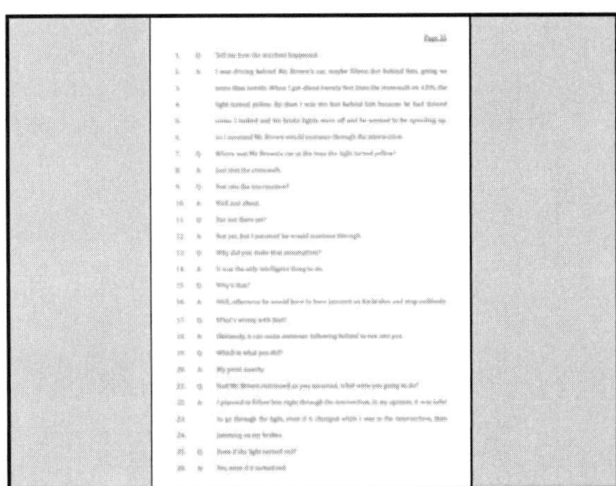

Byrd Transcript p. 35, 1-26   Slide 98

Byrd Video p. 35, 1-26   Slide 99

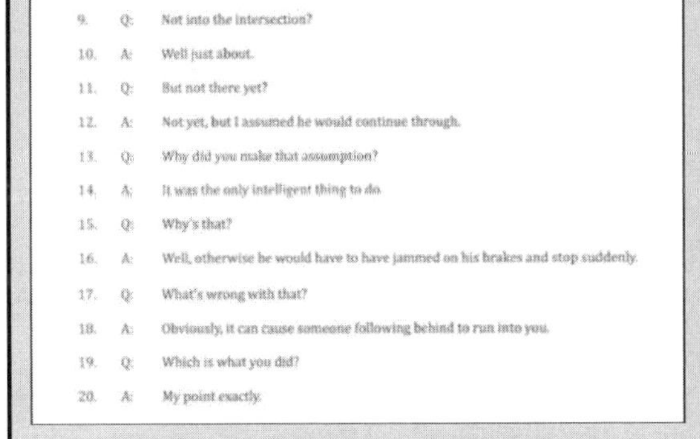

Byrd Transcript p. 35, 7-20   Slide 100

Byrd Video p. 35, 7-20   Slide 101

Byrd Q & A Reveal p. 35, 7-20 Slide 102

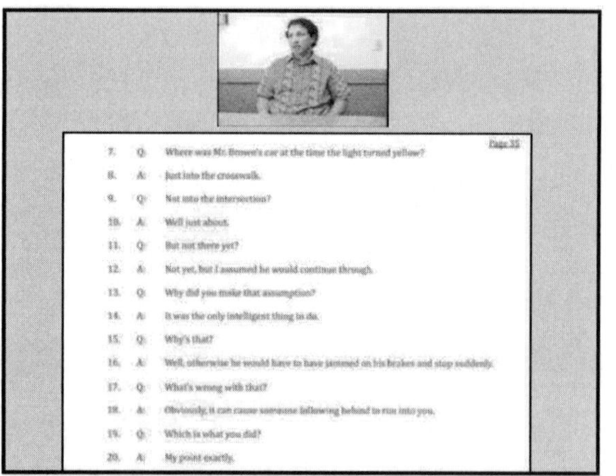

Byrd Q & A Reveal p. 35, 7-20   Slide 103

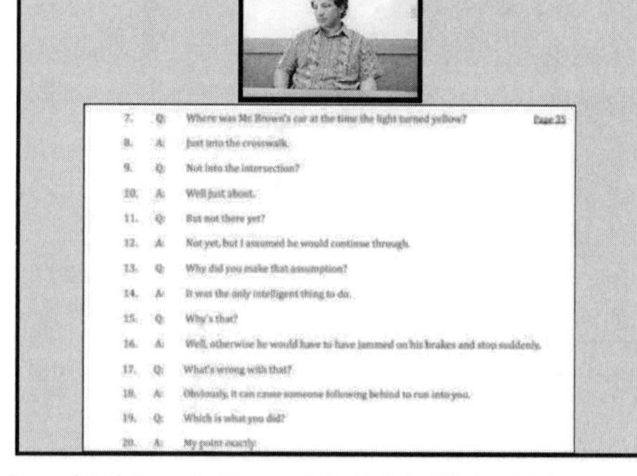

Byrd Video & Tr. p. 35, 7-20 Slide 104

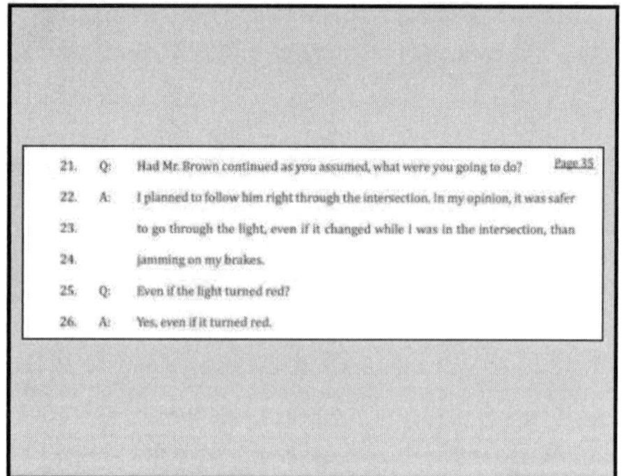

Byrd Transcript p. 35, 21-26   Slide 105

Byrd Video p. 35, 21-26   Slide 106

Byrd Q & A Reveal p. 35, 21-26   Slide 107

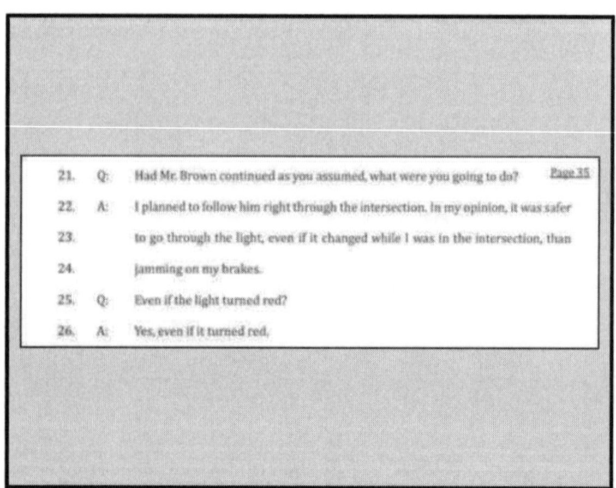

Byrd Q & A Reveal p. 35, 21-26 Slide 108

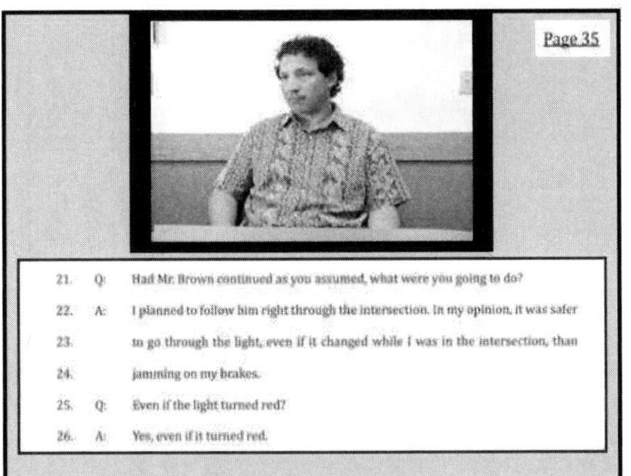

Byrd Video & Tr. p. 35, 21-26   Slide 109

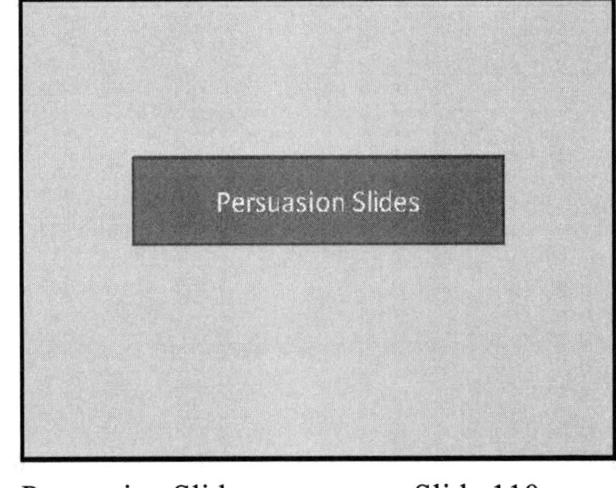

Persuasion Slides   Slide 110

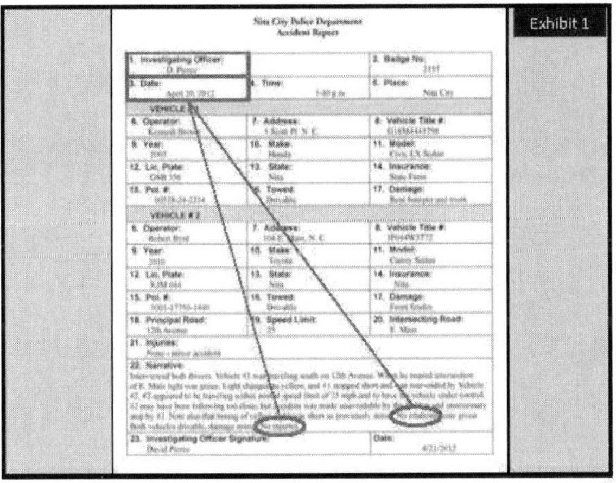

Slide 111

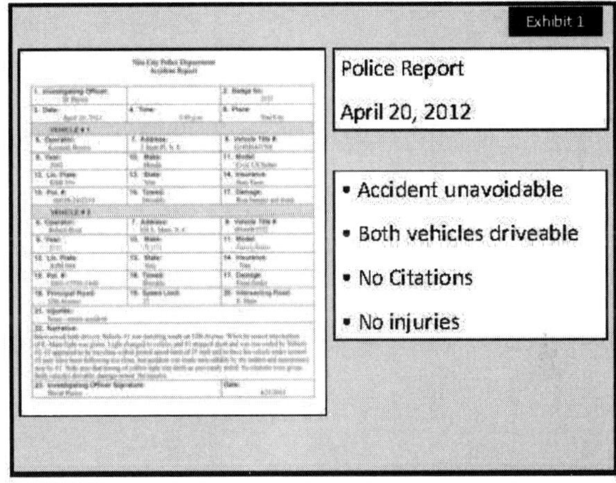

Slide 112

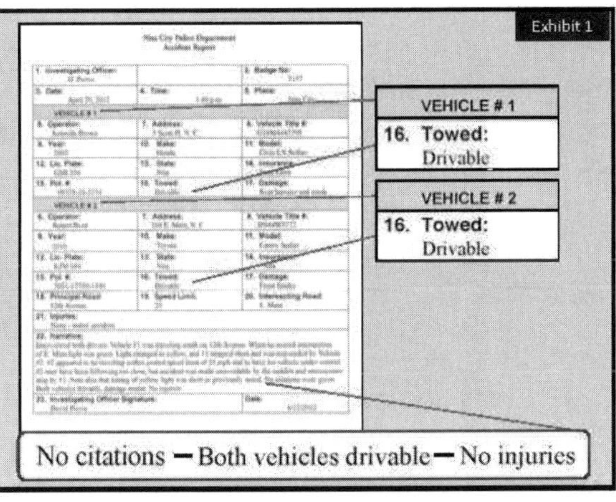

Slide 113

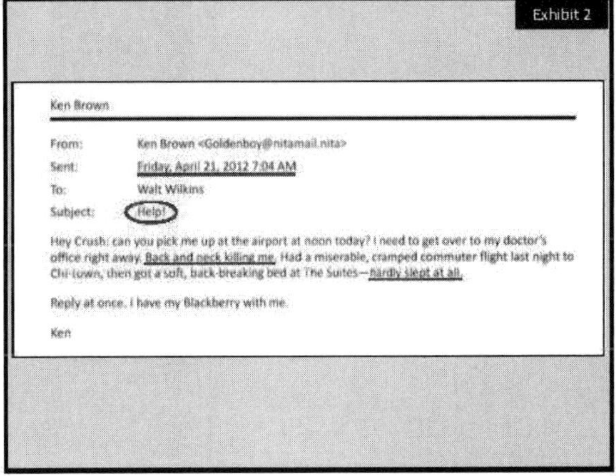

Slide 114

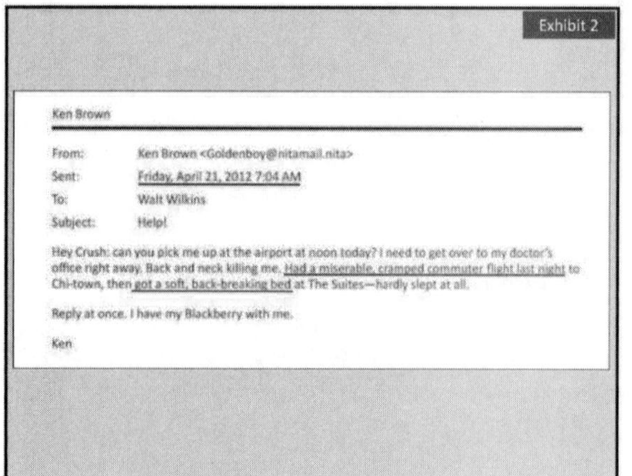

Slide 115

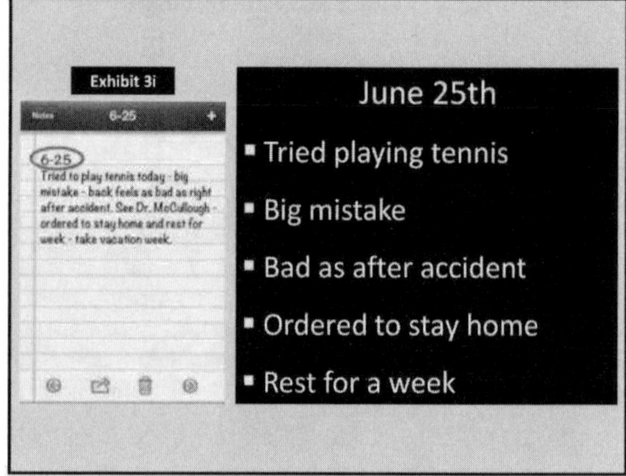

Slide 116

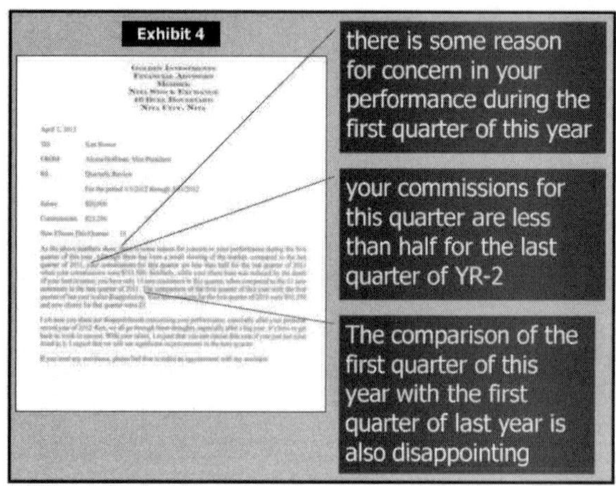

Slide 117

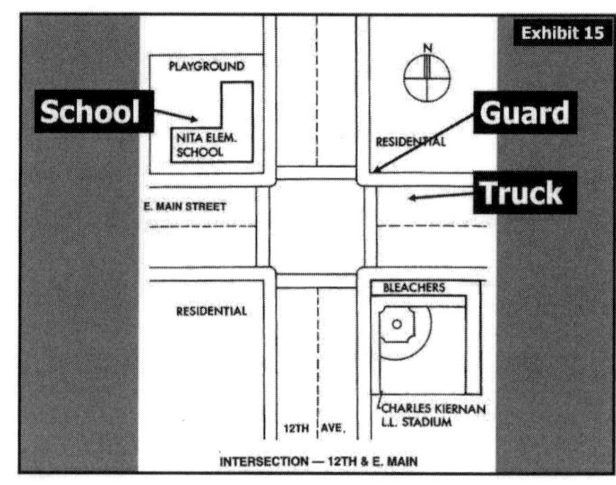

Slide 118

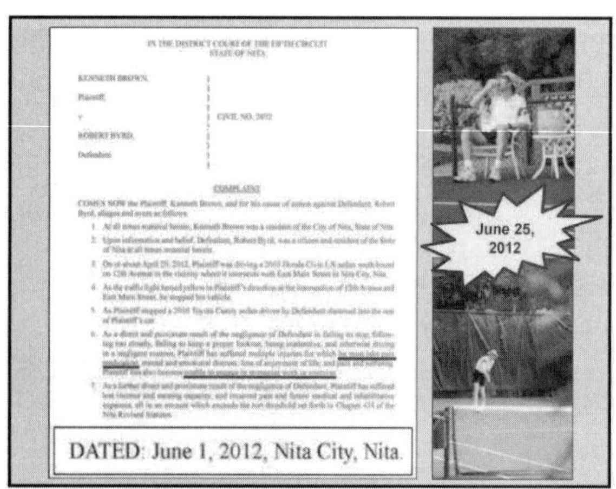

Slide 119

Slide 120

Defendant Byrd

- Light turns yellow
  - Assumes car going thru
  - Plans to go thru himself
  - Looks left and right for traffic
- Car in front stops
- Byrd doesn't stop
- Slams into rear of car in front

Slide 121

Defendant Byrd

- 4 p.m. appointment
- "Cutting it close"
- School zone
- Looking at:
  - Kids on NW corner
  - Guard on NE corner
  - Kids at ice cream truck

Slide 122

Defendant Byrd

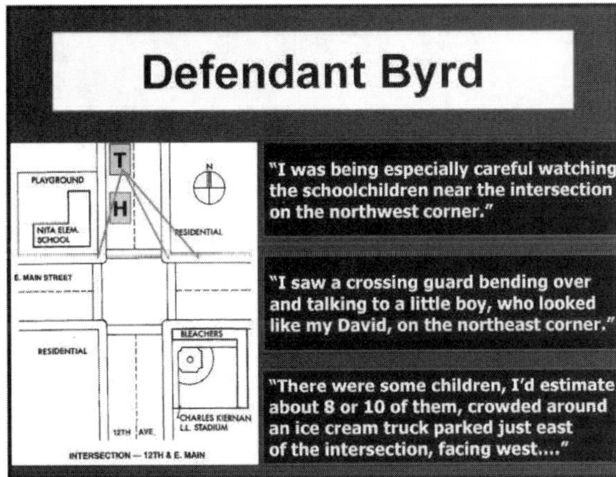

Slide 123

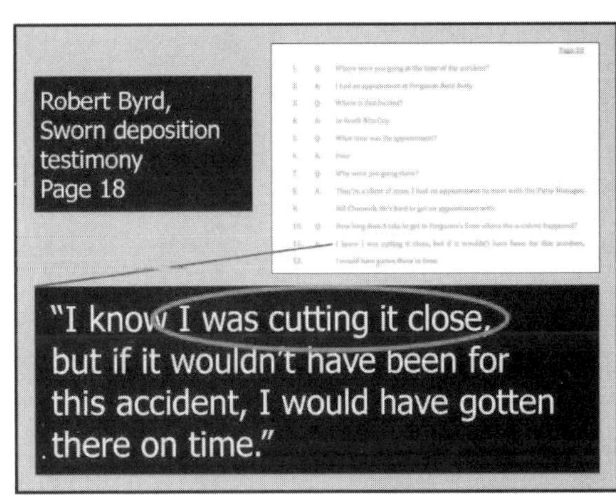

Slide 124

"I was cutting it close"

Robert Byrd, Defendant

Slide 125

The Accident

- ✓ 12th Avenue before Main Street
- ✓ Following Brown's Honda, 20 mph
- ✓ Car at crosswalk, light turns yellow
- ✓ Brown jams brakes, in intersection

Slide 126

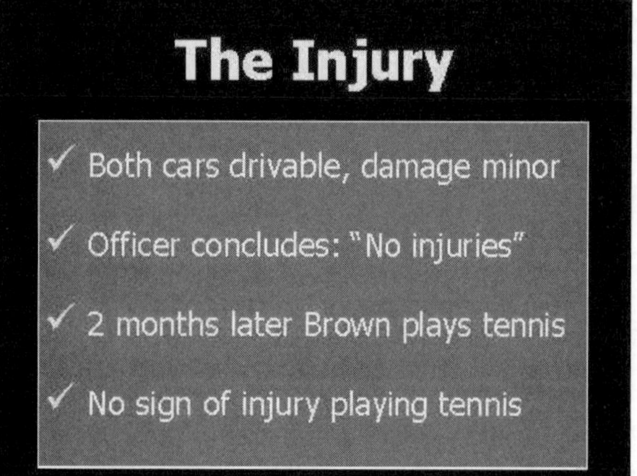

Slide 127

Slide 128

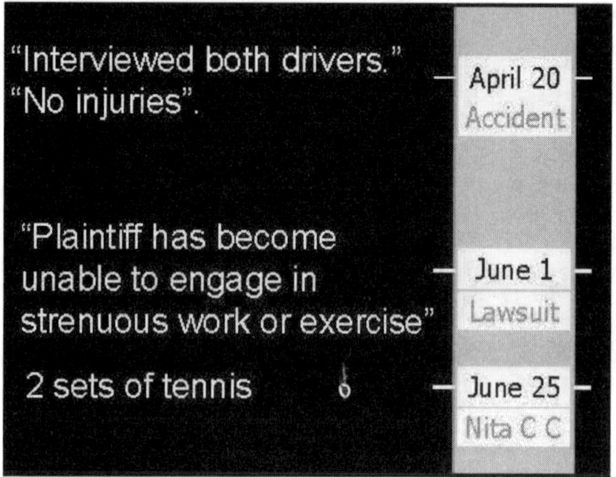

Slide 129

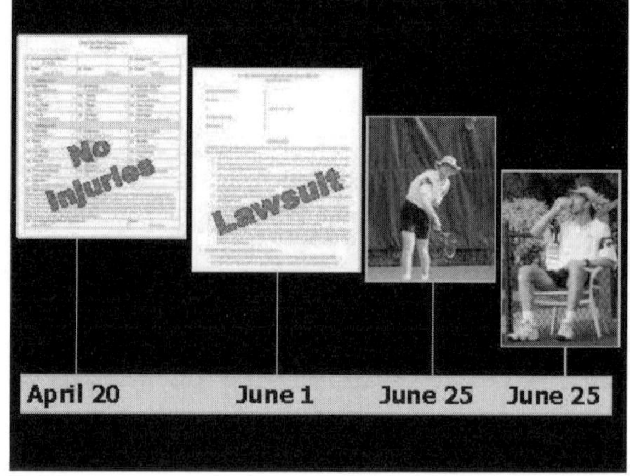

Slide 130

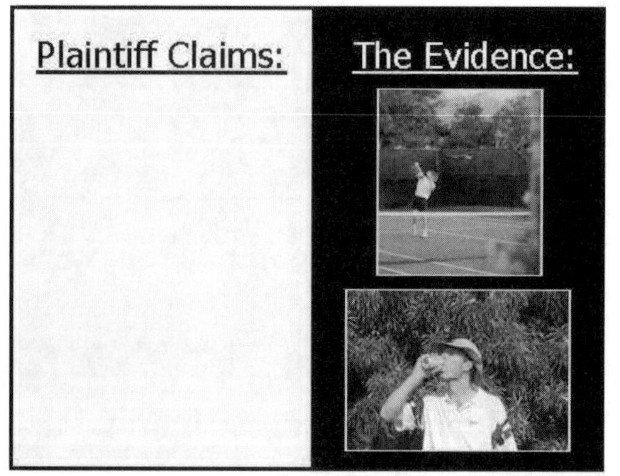

Slide 131

3 month period	January to March, 2011	October to Dec., 2011	January to March, 2012
Commissions	$93,350	$111,500	$23,256
New customers	23	31	11

Slide 132

3 month period	January to March, 2011	October to Dec., 2011	January to March, 2012
Commissions	$93,350	$111,500	$23,256
New customers	23	31	11

Slide 133

Slide 134

Slide 135